The
Hidden Face of
MANET

Photograph of Édouard Manet by Nadar.

The
Hidden Face of
MANET

An investigation of the artist's working processes

Juliet Wilson Bareau

with an introductory essay by
John House

THE BURLINGTON MAGAZINE
1986

Exhibition presented by the Burlington Magazine,
at the Courtauld Institute Galleries, London
23rd April to 15th June 1986

Lenders to the exhibition

Stedelijk Museum, Amsterdam, and Dr. F. F. R. Koenigs
The Walters Art Gallery, Baltimore
Szépmüvészeti Múzeum, Budapest
The Art Institute of Chicago
Ny Carlsberg Glyptotek, Copenhagen
The Burrell Collection, Glasgow Museums and Art Galleries
Trustees of the British Museum, London
Home House Trustees, Courtauld Institute Galleries, London
Trustees of the National Gallery, London
Private collection, London
Nasjonalgalleriet, Oslo
Visitors of the Ashmolean Museum, Oxford
Bibliothèque Nationale, Paris
Cabinet des Dessins, Musée du Louvre, Paris
Musée d'Orsay – Galeries du Jeu de Paume, Paris
Museum Boymans-van Beuningen, Rotterdam

© Juliet Wilson Bareau and The Burlington Magazine

ISBN 0 9511350 0 7

Exhibition designed by Robin Wade Design Associates

Catalogue and exhibition graphics designed by Kevin Shenton

Printed by Jolly & Barber Ltd, Rugby, Warwickshire

Contents

Preface
by Neil MacGregor

This exhibition has an unusual history. As Juliet Wilson Bareau explains in her Introduction, it grew from a conviction that the central element of print connoisseurship, the meticulous examination of a work through its successive 'states', could yield valuable results if applied to certain kinds of paintings – especially those where the artist wrestled with the subject on the canvas itself and transposed works from one medium to another, before finally reaching resolution or giving up. Her energy has been admirable and unremitting. Her results are essentially the fruit of looking: looking again and again, looking with the eye and with every available technological device, and then going back to look once more.

The sequences which emerge form a narrative of great interest. It is the story of how the *Déjeuner sur l'herbe*, *Olympia*, the Mannheim *Maximilian* and the *Bar at the Folies-Bergère* came to be what they are. It is also the story of what else Manet considered making them into, but did not. And that allows us to approach with greater confidence questions such as those explored by John House in his catalogue essay concerning Manet's meaning and intentions.

If investigating Manet has been our main aim, it has not been our only one. The public is at present being asked to supplement the insufficient Government funds for the rehousing in Somerset House of the Courtauld Institute of Art, its libraries and laboratories, paintings and drawings. Without the closest contact between art historians and conservators, without frequent discussion over the objects themselves, this investigation of Manet would hardly have been possible. We hope that the exhibition will thus draw attention to one of the Courtauld's remarkable strengths, its combination, unique in Europe, of a teaching institute, great collections and a pioneering technology department.

All exhibitions depend on a great number of collaborators, but this one surely more than most. Every museum we approached for technological information responded with unstinting generosity. Paintings have been removed from frames, X-rayed and re-X-rayed, and the results shared with such open-handedness that this has been in a real sense an international endeavour. Lenders, both private and public, have been unfailingly generous.

A few special debts of gratitude must be mentioned. Our requests for X-radiographs of paintings in the Collection of the Musée d'Orsay at the Jeu de Paume met with exceptional cooperation from the Director of the Laboratoire de Recherche des Musées de France and his staff. The Technology Department at the Courtauld Institute, and in particular Robert Bruce-Gardiner, shouldered the heavy burden of dealing with the very large number of X-ray films from Paris and elsewhere. The Director of the Courtauld Institute of Art and the Director of the Courtauld Institute Galleries have allowed us to use and to disrupt for some time the Institute's Galleries. The Samuel H. Kress Foundation provided generous financial support for the printing of this catalogue and for the symposium held on 22nd April. The slender staff of The Burlington Magazine, above all Gillian Craig and Irène Logan, shouldered the many extra burdens with unflagging enthusiasm and good cheer. To them, and to those listed below, all involved in the exhibition would like to say thank you: Glenny Alfsen, Eve Alonso, Roseline Bacou, Madeleine Barbin, Laure

Beaumont, D. W. A. L. Beeren, Huguette Berès, Segolène Bergeon, Knut Berg, MM. Bernheim-Jeune, Elizabeth Binckley, Henrik Bjerre, David Bomford, William Bradford, Allen Braham, Robert Bruce-Gardiner, Aviva Burnstock, Mary Bustin, William Clarke, W. H. Crouwel, G.-P. and M. Dauberville, Rini M. Dippel, Roland Dorn, Douglas Druick, Lise Duclos, Pamela England, Lola Faillant-Dumas, Dennis Farr, Manfred Fath, Robin Feathersone, Jay M. Fisher, Suzanne Folds McCullagh, Anne-Birgitte Fonsmark, Jacques Foucart, Teréz Gerszi, Judit Geskó, E. Melanie Gifford, Catherine Goeres, Ian Goodison, Antony Griffiths, Gisela Helmkampf, Françoise Jestaz, F. Koenigs, Michel Laclotte, Annick Lautraite, Michael Levey, Jack Ligot, Christopher Lloyd, Anthony Lousada, Magne Malmanger, Caroline Mathieu, A. W. F. Meij, Ferenc Merényi, Pierre Michel, André Miquel, Maria Gabriela Mizes, Hans Edvard Nørregård-Nielsen, Nicholas Penny, Elizabeth Pile, Leif Einar Plahter, Jurrie A. Poot, Andrée Pouderoux, Pat Read, Stephen Rees-Jones, Jean-Paul Rioux, John Rowlands, Arlette Serullaz, Kevin Shenton, Alistair Smith, Michel Solier, Mary Solt, Lisbeth Stähelin, Margaret Stewart, Peter Sutton, Miklós Szabó, Martyn Tillier, Philip S. Vainker, Hubertus Falkner von Sonnenburg, Daniel Wildenstein, Heather Wilson, Michael Wilson, and the staff at Jolly & Barber, Howard Thomas Photographic and Sovereign Graphics.

1. **11.** Seated bather, with left arm raised. c.1858–60. Red chalk.
   26.6 by 23cm. (The Art Institute of Chicago). Fig.36.
2. **25.** Reclining nude. c.1857–59. Red chalk. 24.7 by 45.7cm.
   (Musée du Louvre, Cabinet des Dessins, Paris). Fig.51.
3. **1.** Sketch for *La nymphe surprise*. c.1858–60. Panel. 35.5 by 46cm.
   Inscribed *E.Manet*. (Nasjonalgalleriet, Oslo). Fig.20.

4. **45.** *Au café*. Signed and dated 1878. 77 by 83cm.
(Sammlung Oskar Reinhart 'Am Römerholz', Winterthur).
Fig. 81.

6. **54.** *Café-concert*. c.1878–80. Signed *Manet*. 47.5 by 39.2cm.
(The Walters Art Gallery, Baltimore). Fig. 94.

5. **46.** *Coin de café-concert*. 1877–79. Signed and dated 1878 (or
1879). 98 by 79cm. (The National Gallery, London). Fig. 82.

7. **49** *La serveuse de bocks*. c.1878–80. Inscribed *E. Manet*.
77.5 by 65cm. (Musée d'Orsay – Galeries du Jeu de Paume,
Paris). Fig. 85.

8. **60.** Sketch for *Un bar aux Folies-Bergère*. 1881.
47 by 56cm. (Stedelijk Museum, Amsterdam;
on loan from Dr.F.F.R.Koenigs). Fig.102.

9. **62.** *Un bar aux Folies-Bergère*. Signed and
dated 1882. 96 by 130cm.
(Courtauld Institute Galleries, London).
Fig.104.

10. **35.** Sketch for *The execution of Maximilian*. 1868–69/1879?
Signed and dated *Manet 1867*. (Ny Carlsberg Glyptotek,
Copenhagen). Fig. 69.
11. **37** *The execution of Maximilian*. Third version. 1868–69/1879?
Signed and dated *19 Juin 1867*. 252 by 305 cm.
(Städtische Kunsthalle, Mannheim). Fig. 71.

Manet's Naïveté by John House

Critics and historians have rarely agreed on how to deal with Manet's art. In his own lifetime, hostile critics saw his paintings as the denial of true painting and its rules, whereas for his supporters they were a stream of life and light, flooding across the artifices of studio and Salon art. The preoccupations of recent historians have been very different; they have tended to focus on two aspects: on his so-called visual 'sources', and on attempts to decode the meaning of his paintings. The search for specific sources from past art for individual elements in Manet's paintings has at times become a sort of competition between historians, as ever more works of art have been brought into play as possible fuel for Manet's picture-making; but this focus on particular elements and particular comparisons has tended to obstruct discussions of the whole paintings whose parts are said to have been 'influenced'. In the search for meanings, the paintings have been presented as ever more complex programmes – either as philosophical allegories, or as documentaries whose 'real' meaning only the most dogged social historian can unravel.[1]

The art-historical industry has certainly increased our information about aspects of Manet's art, but it has produced little agreement on how to approach the paintings themselves. Moreover, it has diverted attention from a sustained study of their original contexts: the process of their physical making, their presentation alongside other pictures in the exhibitions where they were first shown, and the critical debates which grew up around them. The present exhibition, *The Hidden Face of Manet*, concentrates primarily on the first of these, on the artist's working processes, while this essay focuses more on the other two, and seeks to examine two questions: how do we locate Manet's own strategy as a painter of paintings for public exhibitions? and how was it that works which, to one camp, seemed the negation of painting and its rules could, to the other, seem like the revelation of the 'real world' in painting? These questions are in fact inseparable; for his own strategy was conditioned by the ways in which critics classified and discussed paintings. And discussion of this strategy in turn depends on an understanding of his working methods – on the protracted processes of rethinking and refinement by which he distilled his multifarious initial ideas and projects for pictures into the paintings which he completed for public exhibition during his lifetime.

Realist enterprises justify themselves by claims to depict just what the artist sees. But it is never adequate to discuss these enterprises in terms of their degrees of realism, as if they approximated more or less closely to some objective truthfulness. Any painting involves an act of transformation in order to recreate visual experience in terms of line, form and colour on a two-dimensional surface, and to make this translation the painter has to find a framework, a set of codes, within the artificial limitations of the surface and the media used. These frameworks and codes belong to the art of painting, and can only relate in the most oblique way, by convention, to actual perceptions of the world around us – perceptions in time and space, with binocular vision. Moreover, the decision of what to select and how to present it necessarily involves priorities and values. The different ways in which the painters encoded 'reality' in their paintings in the nineteenth century were the physical expression of a wide range of social and ideological viewpoints.

Manet sought 'sincerity' in his paintings, and 'believed that one was not an artist if one was not a primitive';[2] Zola emphasised the *'naïveté'* of his vision, and Manet's associates, Baudelaire and Champfleury, also insisted on the need for the true artist to seek *'naïveté'*.[3] But all ideas of naïveté and the primitive are themselves cultural, not natural. The very concept of innocence presupposes knowledge; the myth of the Garden of Eden makes sense only with prior knowledge of the Fall, and of the Judaeo-Christian distinction between good and evil. Likewise all quests for naïveté and the primitive demand a historical definition, as the antithesis of, and a reaction against, the conceptions of knowledge which are dominant in a particular society or culture, If one characterises a production from outside one's own culture as naïve or primitive, one is signalling the absence of those qualities which, within one's culture, reflect dominant notions of knowledge and skill. It was thus that Baudelaire first reacted to Japanese prints in 1861, calling them *'Images d'Epinal* from Japan', by analogy with the qualities which he and Champfleury found in French popular prints.[4] In seeking a return to naïveté for oneself, the whole nature of that quest will be conditioned by the values of culture and skill which are being repudiated. Alternative frameworks have to be set up, but in order to understand these alternatives, one must define what they are set up as alternatives *to* – what values they seek to negate or subvert. This self-conscious quest for naïveté is just as calculated, just as much the product of knowing artifice, as the conventions which are being rejected.

Zola realised this in 1867, writing that Manet painted 'in a way that is wholly naïve, yet wholly thought out'; forgetting so-called rules, he 'places himself in front of nature with naïveté'. In 1846, Baudelaire cryptically defined naïveté as 'knowledge [of one's craft] giving the principal rôle to temperament', and enlarged on this idea in *Le peintre de la vie moderne*, his essay on Constantin Guys written in 1859–60: 'Genius is childhood recovered at will, a childhood now equipped for self expression with manhood's capacities and a power of analysis which enables it to order the mass of raw material which it has involuntarily accumulated.' Champfleury defined naïveté at some length in an invocation to contemporary artists in 1869, in the introduction to his *Histoire de l'imagerie populaire*, urging them to forget their accumulated knowledge of the art of the past; 'naïveté cannot be learned; it comes from the heart, not the head'; it must be cultivated by ignoring fashion and easy success, and seeking out one's own simple, original vision.[5]

In 1876, Mallarmé described Manet's approach to art in very similar terms:

> Each time he begins a picture, says he, he plunges headlong into it, and feels like a man who knows that his surest plan to learn how to swim safely, is, dangerous as it may seem, to throw himself into the water. One of his habitual aphorisms then is that no one should paint a landscape and a figure by the same process, with the same knowledge, or in the same fashion; nor what is more, even two landscapes or two figures. Each work should be a new creation of the mind. The hand, it is true, will conserve some of its acquired secrets of manipulation, but the eye should forget all else it has seen, and learn anew from the lesson before it. It should abstract itself from memory, seeing only that which it looks upon, and that as for the first time; and the hand should become an impersonal abstraction guided only by the will, oblivious of all previous cunning.

Mallarmé went on to describe Manet's gradual process of self emancipation from the past and from 'affectation and style'.[6]

In each of these accounts, the artist has to emancipate himself from the whole residue of conventional knowledge; but inevitably the definition of freedom and naïveté will be determined by the terms and frameworks of the knowledge which is being rejected. In looking at Manet's art, we have to define the conventional cultural codes from which he sought to free himself; it was his rejection and subversion of these which proved to his detractors that he could not paint, and at the same time led his supporters to view his work as a truthful, natural form of painting. Manet's preface, written in the third person, to the catalogue of his 1867 one-man exhibition helps us focus more closely on the cultural context of his enterprise:

> The artist does not say today: come and see works without faults, but: come and see sincere works. It is sincerity which gives them a character which makes them seem like a protest, although the painter has thought only of rendering his own impression. M. Manet has never wanted to protest. On the contrary the protests have been against him, and he did not expect this; they arose because there is a traditional way of teaching forms, methods and aspects of painting, and because those who have been brought up to believe in those principles will admit no others. . . . Apart from their formulae, nothing is worth anything, and they become not only critics but active opponents.[7]

Though Manet does not here explicitly define his 'sincerity' by reference to the traditional methods he has rejected, the close conjunction of the two in his account shows that he saw a direct relationship between them.

The site of this relationship, moreover, was a very specific one, the Paris Salon. It was on the Salon walls, amid the other exhibits, that Manet's principal pictures were intended to be seen, and it was within the verbal frameworks of the Salon critics that they were classified and mediated for their waiting public. It is in the context of the Salon, too, that we can best understand the remarkable diversity of Manet's exhibition pictures, for he explored and rethought very many of the varied types of painting currently most popular at the Salon – religious painting, the pastoral, the nude, portraiture, peasantry, genre painting and so on. Antonin Proust remembered Manet expostulating against the critics in 1882:

> The imbeciles! They have never stopped telling me that I am inconsistent: they couldn't say anything more flattering. It has always been my ambition not to remain consistent, not to re-do, the next day, what I had done the day before, but constantly to find my inspiration from some new aspect, and to seek to produce a new note.[8]

However, it was still the frameworks of the Salon which shaped his choice of subjects for his exhibition pictures, and it is in that context that we can best understand their conception and reception: the frameworks of representation which Manet evolved, and the verbal rhetoric of naturalness and naïveté which grew up around his pictures, make most sense when viewed as explicit rejections of academic conventions.

In order to understand the forms which Manet's paintings took, we must spell out the most central of these conventions. Three points seem crucial. First, the scene depicted should be self-contained and complete in itself; it should not implicitly continue beyond the margins of the picture, nor should the figures within the painting actively implicate the viewer, by looking out into our space. Second, the action or grouping should be legible to the viewer. There was a whole range of conventions available to the painter for directing the viewer's attention to the salient points of a picture: by the arrangement of the figures, their gestures and their facial expression; by the use of intelligible attributes, whether naturalistic or symbolic, and by the way these objects are related to the figures; by the use of colour or the brush to throw emphasis on the salient parts of the picture; and by the painting's title (and other attendant texts, like the extracts from literary sources often included in the Salon *livret*). Third, Salon painting still normally conformed to the traditional hierarchy of genres in painting, whereby history, religion and mythology had a higher status, and, as 'significant' subjects, could be treated on a larger scale and in a more ambitious way than more trivial themes like everyday genre and landscape.

1. *Le vieux musicien*, by Édouard Manet. 1862. 187.4 by 248.3 cm. (National Gallery of Art, Washington, D.C.)
2. *À l'ombre des bosquets chante un jeune poète*, by Ernest Meissonier. 1853. 18 by 21 cm. (Wallace Collection, London.)
3. *Le fifre*, by Édouard Manet. 1866. 160 by 98 cm. (Musée d'Orsay – Galeries du Jeu de Paume, Paris.)
4. *Le joueur de flûte*, by Ernest Meissonier. 1858. 33 by 22 cm. (Present whereabouts unknown.)

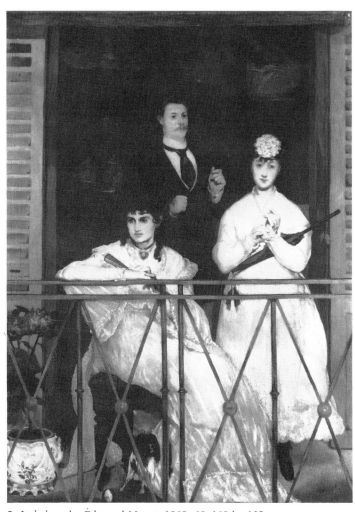

6. *La visite*, by Alfred Stevens. Exhibited at
the Paris Exposition Universelle, 1867.
(Dimensions and present whereabouts
unknown.)

5. *Le balcon*, by Édouard Manet. 1868–69. 169 by 125cm.
(Musée d'Orsay – Galeries du Jeu de Paume, Paris.)

8. *Le vin du curé*, by Ernest Meissonier. 1860.
11.5 by 15.3cm.
(Musée Saint-Denis, Reims).

7. *Le déjeuner*, by Édouard Manet. 1868. 118 by 153.9cm.
(Bayerische Staatsgemäldesammlungen, Munich.)

It was these expectations which underpinned the writings of contemporary art critics, whether they endorsed them or questioned their relevance to modern painting. The difficulties which critics found in dealing with Manet's art highlight the ways in which he systematically transgressed these basic tenets of exhibition painting, both by the illegibility and apparent incompleteness of his subjects, and by the large scale on which he treated 'insignificant' types of subject. Excerpts from contemporary criticism are often used in discussion of individual nineteenth-century paintings, sometimes to elucidate their interpretation, but more often to reveal the critics' failure to understand them. Though such extracts may sometimes be illuminating, their tone and their terms of reference may be puzzling or actively misleading when they are taken out of their original context, as contributions to current debates, amid the mass of art critical writing of the period. The criticism of Manet was surveyed by George Heard Hamilton in 1954, in a book which retains a real importance despite the reservations which many readers in the 1980s will feel about its overall viewpoint. Recently, T. J. Clark has examined the criticism of *Olympia* in depth. From these and other sources, we can sum up the terms in which the contemporary debates around Manet were conducted. A comprehensive survey of the original publications (were this ever made) would doubtless modify and refine certain points, but the general patterns of the arguments are clear.[9]

Few critics gave sustained attention to Manet in his early years. After a moderate initial success with *Espagnol jouant de la guitare* in 1861, he became notorious with the exhibition of *Le bain (Le déjeuner sur l'herbe)* at the Salon des Refusés in 1863 and *Olympia* at the 1865 Salon; but as Clark has shown, even *Olympia* elicited little more than puzzlement or outrage. However, the *Olympia* scandal made him hard to ignore, and Zola's pamphlet on Manet of 1867, the first extended discussion and defence of his art, may have persuaded critics that it deserved more serious treatment. Thereafter it was often discussed at length, even by his opponents, but it is often misleading to categorise individual critics as supporters or opponents, for one and the same writer might defend him one year and condemn him the next. Through the 1870s, though, there seems to be a gradual change in his favour, but many of the old critical stereotypes were still reiterated in the early 1880s.[10]

These stereotypes were firmly established by the mid 1860s: his paintings were incompetent in drawing, colour and composition; they were incomplete; and the artist chose ugly types, unworthy of presentation in art. Such criticisms view Manet's art straightforwardly as the antithesis of conventional standards of manual skill and moral value in art. A typical, though unusually witty, example was Louis Leroy's review of 1868, in which the pictures themselves declare their positions, and Manet's *Portrait of Emile Zola* comments:

> At the end of yesterday's session I forgot to mention half a dozen points upon which my lack of belief is complete: I deny form, colour, line, composition, I deny common sense . . . I deny virtue . . . I deny distinction . . . I deny everybody . . . I deny poetry . . . I deny truth . . . I deny civilisation.[11]

Rather more specific is a series of criticisms of Manet's failure to differentiate his figures from the other parts of his composition. Thoré raised this objection in 1863, and it was taken up by Paul Mantz in 1868 and by Castagnary as late as 1875, but it was Thoré, again, who gave it its fullest formulation, in 1868:

> When he has placed on his canvas 'the *tache* of colour' which a figure or an object makes on its natural surroundings, he gives up. Don't ask him for anything more, for the moment. But he will sort this out later, when he decides to give their relative value to the essential parts of human beings. His present vice is a sort of pantheism which places no higher value on a head than on a slipper; which sometimes even gives more importance to a bunch of flowers than to a woman's face . . . which paints everything almost uniformly – furniture, carpets, books, costumes, flesh, facial features.[12]

Such comments were all the more pointed from Thoré and Castagnary, both firm supporters of contemporary subject matter in art. Closely connected to this objection was the regular claim that Manet followed the eye alone, and neglected feeling, imagination, soul and brain;[13] again, the argument was that Manet's art lacked the moral and human dimension essential in serious art.

At times, too, his art was more directly contrasted with the conventions of fashionable genre painting, particularly from the later 1860s onwards, when his subjects invited comparison with them. Such comments appeared in favourable and unfavourable commentaries alike. Thus Marius Chaumelin wrote in 1869 that *Le balcon* (Fig. 5) and *Le déjeuner* (Fig. 7) in 1869 'have greatly scandalised the lovers of neat, tidy, sentimental bourgeois painting', criticising their lack of 'expression, sentiment and composition' – prerequisites of such bourgeois art – and praising only certain details and harmonies; the next year Duranty turned this comparison emphatically in Manet's favour, writing of *La leçon de musique* (Fig. 9):

> Against refined, artful painting Manet opposes a systematic naïveté and a scorn of all seductive devices. He places his figures against a dull, slate grey background, as if he was puritanically protesting against the bric-à-brac furnishings which the greater and the lesser *toulmoucherie*, and the still-life painters, heap up for fear of being taken for paupers.[14]

Comparison with the sumptuous domestic interiors in which painters such as Auguste Toulmouche, Alfred Stevens and Gustave de Jonghe (Figs. 6, 12 and 16) placed their anecdotal contemporary genre scenes helps us to focus on the spareness of Manet's picture, and on its physical scale – very large for such a subject. Such comparisons continued throughout Manet's life; in 1875 Junius wrote of his 'eccentric hatred of the banal and the conventional', and as late as 1882 Albert Wolff concluded that 'his hatred of *la peinture frisée et pommadée* often leads him to overshoot the mark'.[15]

More specifically, many of his canvases confronted their commentators with problems of legibility; the human relationships which they presented could not readily be decoded according to the accepted conventions of depicting interaction between figures. For Louis Lagrange in 1861, the canvas exhibited as *Portrait de M. et Mme M.*, but known to represent Manet's parents, was a travesty of filial duty: 'To [the realist painter] nothing is sacred: M. Manet tramples on even more hallowed affections.'[16] Puzzlement at the meaning of his figure groupings came to the fore when *Le balcon* (Fig. 5) and *Le déjeuner* (Fig. 7) were shown in 1869. Gautier playfully tried to make sense of *Le déjeuner*: 'But why these weapons on the table? Is it the luncheon given before or after a duel? We don't know.' Mantz had similar problems with *Le balcon*, and gave some clue to the ways in which a reading of the figures might be sought:

> One doesn't quite know what these good people are doing on the balcony, and the German critics, curious about the philosophical meaning of things, would be very hard put to understand or explain the content. The accentuation of a type, the characterisation of a feeling or an idea, would be sought in vain in this painting devoid of thought.[17]

Both subjects baffled Castagnary, and led him to a valuable definition of the qualities which he felt a genre subject ought to present:

> In looking at this *Déjeuner* . . . I see, on a table where coffee has been served, a half-peeled lemon and some fresh oysters; these objects hardly go together. Why were they put there? . . . Just as Manet assembles, for the mere pleasure of astonishing, objects which should be mutually incompatible, so he arranges his people at random without any reason or meaning for the composition. The result is uncertainty and often obscurity in thought. What is the young man of the *Déjeuner* doing, the one who is seated in the foreground and who

seems to be looking at the public? . . . Where is he? In the dining room? If so, having his back to the table, he has the wall between himself and us, and his position is inexplicable. On the *Balcon* I see two women, one of them very young. Are they sisters? Is this a mother and daughter? I don't know. And then one has seated herself apparently just to enjoy the view of the street; the other is putting on her gloves as if she were just about to go out. This contradictory attitude bewilders me. . . . A feeling for form, for fitness are indispensable. Neither the writer nor the painter can neglect them. Like characters in a comedy, so in a painting each figure must be in its place, play its part, and so contribute to the expression of the general idea. Nothing arbitrary and nothing superfluous, such is the law of every artistic composition.[18]

Castagnary's comments about the missing front wall in *Le déjeuner* are at first sight particularly puzzling, for the conventions of comedy, which he invokes, demand just this – the replacement of the front wall of the room in which the action takes place by the proscenium arch. However, his complaint may make more sense when seen in the context of comedy's expectations of unified action confined within the stage space, where the space between stage and audience acts as a sort of inviolable membrane, which can be broken only at the moments when one of the characters steps aside from the action to address the audience directly. In Manet's painting, the boy's gaze looks out and beyond the viewer, quite without explanation of where it is directed or how it relates to the action (or rather inaction) within the painting; at one and the same time it engages our space and thwarts our attempts to read it. With *Le chemin de fer* (Fig. 11) in 1874, similar uncertainties about the nature of the subject and the action led Duvergier de Hauranne to ask: 'Is Manet's *Le chemin de fer* a double portrait or a subject picture? . . . we lack the information to solve the problem; we are even more uncertain about the young girl, for this would be a portrait seen from the rear.' In 1882, the cause for concern was the mirror in *Un bar aux Folies-Bergère* (Fig. 104, Col. ill. 9), and its failure to provide an intelligible reflection of the foreground scene.[19]

Why did Manet treat his subjects in these disconcerting ways? For many critics it was a case of simple incompetence, but others, for all their reservations, provided more positive explanations. It was perhaps Zola's 1867 article which set the tone of most of these, by its insistence on the primacy of *taches* of colour over ideas in Manet's art. In 1869, both Mantz and Castagnary followed this line: 'Let's admit that it's about combining colours', wrote Mantz; 'Manet possesses, in the highest degree, a feeling for the colour-giving *tache*', explained Castagnary.[20] In 1882, Chesneau summed up Manet's virtues as lying 'in the accurate vision of things and their colouring, their luminous vibration, and their fleeting, fugitive appearance', rather than in the search for a 'distinguished subject'. As T. J. Clark has pointed out, such criticism marks the emergence of concerns which were to become dominant in modernist writing.[21]

However, explanations such as these did not become dominant during Manet's lifetime. Moreover, they bypass the issue of the pictures' apparent thematic incoherence, of their transgression of the standards of 'form and fitness' which Castagnary had laid down in 1869: how far was the illegibility of the pictures a central part of their artistic programme? In 1873, Marc de Montifaud (pseudonym of Marie-Amélie Chartroule de Montifaud) suggested that Manet's rejection of these conventions was calculated, in her discussion of *Le bon bock*: 'Don't demand of the picture preordained rules of composition; the author doesn't understand them or doesn't want to understand them, but only the free and dominant note that each object has in nature. Manet doesn't look for the soul of a face, but rather for its general appearance.'[22] Mallarmé explained in 1876 in more positive terms why composition played no part in Manet's search for atmospheric truth: 'As a rule the grouping of modern persons does not suggest [composition], and for this reason our painter is pleased to dispense with it, and at the same time to avoid both affectation and style.' Manet replaced these conventional notions of composition with 'natural perspective', which, with the help of examples such as Japanese art, allowed him to find a framework for his depiction of the modern world; this, Mallarmé declared, was based on the way in which Manet used the picture frame to cut the forms in his pictures.[23] These de-composed groups, and this 'natural perspective', were thus defined by reference to conventional modes of picture making, and were presented as a deliberate rejection of them.

We gain further insight into Manet's alertness to the conventions of Salon painting from a story recounted by Antonin Proust after the painter's death: 'Alfred Stevens had painted a picture of a woman drawing aside a curtain. At the bottom of this curtain there was a feather duster which played the part of the useless adjective in a fine phrase of prose or the padding in a well-turned verse. "It's quite clear," said Manet, "this woman's waiting for the valet".'[24] It was just this sort of genre subject, incorporating details and signs that invited narrative reading, that Manet deliberately avoided, and this potential legibility that he subverted in his own paintings, by presenting groupings of figures and details which defied such interpretation.

When we survey Manet's career as a whole, there is a clear break around 1865. Before then, his major canvases all make more or less clear reference to various old-master prototypes or archetypes, though from the start his subjects and the ways he tackled them also relate closely to contemporary Salon painting. It may, indeed, have been his experience of Velázquez's art in Madrid in 1865 which enabled him to see how modernity could be seamlessly fused with tradition. Thereafter, references to the past become less specific, and they virtually disappear after 1870, but throughout his career the paintings he submitted to the Salon retained equally close links to the genres and conventions of Salon painting.

Antonin Proust's reminiscences of Manet's student days (for all their hindsight, virtually our only evidence of these years) reiterate Manet's early hostility to history painting, and show him holding up his experience of the outside world as the antithesis to standard studio practices, revealing their artificiality: insisting on a model posing *clothed*, scorning historical costume and the niceties of exhibition finish and studio lighting.[25]

Yet his early canvases were conceived overtly in old-master terms. Piecemeal pinpointing of particular 'sources' from past art for individual figures is rarely convincing; often several equally plausible comparisons can be found for a single figure, which suggests that Manet was looking to generic figure types rather than to particular examples.[26] But, more important, this process diverts attention from the crucial issue of how the elements were combined in the picture in question: like words in a sentence, it is the combination that generates meanings.

Manet's working methods reveal the constant process of manipulation and recombination by which he arrived at his finished paintings. The evidence displayed in the present exhibition shows how wide a range of external stimuli were assimilated in some way into the various projects involving nude female figures which he explored between 1859 and 1863; he investigated and discarded many different combinations of figures and several potential subjects for his canvases before fixing on his final solutions. These experiments were made with constant reference to examples from past art, yet the finished productions recreated these prototypes in ways which engaged more closely with current concerns in Salon painting.

Manet's transformation of Titian's Urbino *Venus* into the image of a modern prostitute in *Olympia* (Fig. 30) gained its point in the Salon as a rejection of the conventions of such Salon Venuses as Cabanel's 1863 Gold Medal winner, *La naissance de Vénus*.[27] In *Le bain (Le déjeuner sur l'herbe)* (Fig. 19) his combination of the idea of the Giorgione-Titian *Concert champêtre* with a group from Marcantonio's *Judgment of Paris* engraving seemed to its public a startling travesty of the idea of

10. *La leçon de lecture*, by Auguste
Toulmouche. 1865. 36.5 by 27.5 cm.
(Museum of Fine Arts, Boston.)

9. *La leçon de musique,* by Édouard Manet. 1870. 140 by 173 cm.
(Museum of Fine Arts, Boston.)

12. *La petite paresseuse*, by Gustave de Jonghe.
1867. (Dimensions and present whereabouts
unknown.)

11. *Le chemin de fer*, by Édouard Manet. 1873. 93.3 by 114.5 cm.
(National Gallery of Art, Washington, D.C.)

14. *Meeting in a riverside café* (original title
    unknown), by James Tissot. c.1869.
    40.6 by 53.3 cm. (Private collection.)

13. *Chez le père Lathuille*, by Édouard Manet. 1879. 92 by 112 cm.
    (Musée des Beaux-Arts, Tournai.)

16. *Flirtation*, by Auguste Toulmouche
    (reproduced from an engraving). 1876.
    (Dimensions and present whereabouts
    unknown.)

15. *Dans la serre*, by Édouard Manet. 1879. 115 by 150 cm.
    (Nationalgalerie, Berlin.)

the *fête champêtre*: the modern costumes and the uncoordinated gazes of the figures, with the naked woman looking directly at the spectator, made it impossible to envisage the scene as an idyll taking place in a land of make-believe, safely distanced in time or space.[28]

If *Olympia* and *Le bain* were attempts to harness the traditions of the high renaissance to a genuinely modern painting, *Le vieux musicien* of 1862 (Fig. 1) did the same for the 'realists' of the seventeenth century. The picture was shown at Martinet's gallery, not at the Salon. It is possible that at this date Manet felt that such an overt exploration of the 'realist tradition' was not feasible at the Salon in so large and stark a composition. The painting attracted little attention when it was exhibited early in 1863, but recently it has been the focus of much art-historical discussion, ranging from John Richardson's celebrated verdict of 1958 that it proved that 'Manet's sense of design was faulty', to a barrage of potential 'sources' and interpretations.[29] However, the references seem to be generic, not specific, and the relevance of the echoes of Velázquez and the more evident debt to the Le Nain brothers lies in current interest in these artists in realist circles in Paris, and particularly in the way in which the compositional techniques of the Le Nains were described by Champfleury in 1860: 'Their means of composing are anti-academic, avoiding the simplest laws; they do not bother to group their figures. . . . They have taken their search for reality as far as the awkwardness of placing isolated figures in the middle of the canvas; by this they are the fathers of current experiments, and their reputation can only grow.'[30] Again, the 'reality' of their compositions is defined in terms of their rejection of academic convention.

The composition of *Le vieux musicien* is even more fragmented than any by the Le Nains, and its dislocation would have seemed still more evident by comparison with contemporary Salon painting. Schlesinger's *L'enfant volé*, shown at the 1861 Salon, has been uncritically cited as yet another 'source' for Manet's picture, but its unambiguously focused, centralised composition employs all the devices of compositional artifice that Manet rejected.[31] The title of Manet's canvas suggests a further context for it, in other paintings of music-making. In this tradition, running from Raphael's *Parnassus* through to paintings such as Meissonier's *A l'ombre des bosquets chante un jeune poète* (Fig. 2), exhibited in 1853, the music-maker is presented as the focus for a ring of attentive listeners; Manet's musician is placed off-centre, and is not playing, and his companions look in various directions.

These paintings of the early 1860s seem to propose an active dialogue between past and present, whereas in *Le fifre* (Fig. 3), rejected at the 1866 Salon, the references are far less explicit. The example of Velázquez may have helped Manet to see how to float a broadly brushed, crisply contoured figure against a scarcely differentiated background, but the immediate context for the treatment he adopted was paintings such as Meissonier's elaborately uniform soldiers, and his costumed musician figures such as the 1858 *Joueur de flûte* (Fig. 4). Likewise the *Jeune dame en 1866 (La femme au perroquet)*, quizzically gazing at the spectator, and demurely but informally dressed in her dressing gown, is at one and the same time a rejection of the wanton artifice of Courbet's *La femme au perroquet*, exhibited in 1866, and of the modern dress costume piece of fashionable women with their pets.[32] At the other extreme, his one venture into history painting in the later 1860s, *L'exécution de l'Empereur Maximilien*, intended for the 1869 Salon (Fig. 71, Col. ill. 11), undermines the expectations of this type of picture: the royal victim is impassive, his executioners rigid and inexpressive. The body of General Mejía on the left – seemingly just shot – arches back, and his fist is clenched, but Manet avoids throughout the rhetorical gestures and exaggerated facial expressions which were stock-in-trade of contemporary military painting at the Salon. The discrepancy between the treatment which would have been expected of so loaded and poignant a subject and the way in which Manet presented the scene would have seemed very pointed if Manet had been able to exhibit it at the time.[33]

As contemporary critics realised, Manet's modern subjects shown in 1869 brought into sharp focus his refusal to follow the conventions of genre painting and to give his paintings a legible plot. *Le balcon* (Fig. 5) invites comparison with images of fashionable women making a social call such as Stevens's *La visite* (Fig. 6), exhibited in 1867, and *Le déjeuner* (Fig. 7) with many recent paintings of conviviality (e.g. Fig. 8), but in both the signs are contradictory, and cannot be assimilated into a single coherent reading. Their very large scale, and the spareness of their treatment, as in *La leçon de musique* (Fig. 9), shown in 1870, mark out their rejection of *toulmoucherie*.[34] His 1874 exhibit, *Le chemin de fer* (Fig. 11), plays on a related set of expectations: woman with book, suggesting study or meditation; woman with child and book, suggesting education, as in Toulmouche's *La leçon de lecture* of 1865 (Fig. 10). But the formal contrasts and the complete lack of communication between the figures deny these associations. Occasionally in the Salon genre tradition, the poses of two figures may be pulled apart, as in de Jonghe's *La petite paresseuse* (Fig. 12) of 1867, but there the girl's legs remain planted in the mother's embracing skirt, and the space with the book on mother's knee remains open to her once her fit of temperament has abated. Manet allows no such readings, and there is no waiting space on the woman's lap – indeed the oblivious puppy takes the expected place of the child. The title of the picture, *Le chemin de fer*, compounds the oddity, for it signals the background, not the foreground, and an absence, not a presence: the girl is looking into the shapeless puff of smoke left by a train that has passed.

Between 1875 and 1880 Manet exhibited four ambitious canvases of a man and a woman together: *Argenteuil* in 1875, *En bateau* and *Dans la serre* (Fig. 15) in 1879, and *Chez le père Lathuille* (Fig. 13) in 1880. All four titles are uninformative, indicating only the place of the scene, and nothing about the relationship between the couple; and in all the pictures the figures are paired in ways which baulk the viewer. In *Argenteuil* the woman looks impassively at the viewer, taking no notice of the man, all of whose gestures invade her space. There is no interchange between the figures in *En bateau*, and the intelligibility of the subject is further undermined by a change which Manet made during the execution of the picture: originally the rope on the sail ran into the man's right hand; when it was moved to its present position, tied to a belaying pin on the bench, his hand was left unmoved, despite the removal of the only reason for his holding it across his left knee.[35] The focus of the man's attentions in *Chez le père Lathuille* are quite clear, as he encircles the woman and appropriates her glass, though strangely he is crouching without a chair, as if he had only casually paused to flirt with her. Her reactions, though, are quite unclear, since Manet treated the face inexplicitly enough to enable a wide range of possible readings of its expression, in contrast to Tissot's *Meeting in a riverside café* (Fig. 14), in which the young woman's expression is placed directly before the viewer.[36] *Dans la serre* is particularly comparable to Toulmouche's *Flirtation* (Fig. 16), shown at the 1876 Salon, and at first sight the relationships depicted in it can be equally easily read, as the man leans across the back of the bench towards the woman, and their hands, with their wedding rings, almost meet; but her gaze is distant, and we notice that his hand is placed where it is in order to hold a large cigar. Once again, any clear access to the couple's relationship is thwarted.

With *Un bar aux Folies-Bergère* (Fig. 104, Col. ill. 9), exhibited at the Salon of 1882, the evidence of X-rays, displayed in the present exhibition, provides crucial evidence of how deliberately Manet undermined the viewer's expectations, as he transformed the final canvas from the intelligible spatial relationships seen in the study to the logical incomprehensibility of its final state: there is no way that we can reconcile our relationship to the woman who faces us out of the picture with the face-to-face meeting of woman and tophatted man in the reflection. In spatial terms, this is the most glaring of the many inconsistencies and ambiguities which Manet had created in his canvases throughout his career, and it assumes a central rôle in the viewer's experience of the picture.

The discussion so far has focused principally on the context of Manet's paintings at the Paris Salon, in relation to critical writing and to the other paintings shown there. Inevitably an account like that presented here over-simplifies and mis-represents this context, by selecting brief extracts from the criticism, and by presenting particular visual pairings, between a work by Manet and one by another artist, when the verbal and visual context was so unlike this: the commentaries on Manet were embedded in the hundreds of thousands of words each year by which the critics groped for patterns of coherence, amid the diversity of the thousands of canvases displayed at each Salon. But, for all its shortcomings, such an analysis is essential to any understanding of how his paintings carried meaning on their first appearance, and what meanings they carried.

Indeed, this context belongs only to the canvases he sought to show in this vast and multifarious forum; for when he exhibited outside the Salon, in more informal surroundings, he was willing to show smaller paintings, yet more unconventional in composition. Alongside *Le vieux musicien* (Fig.1), very large but blatantly illegible in conventional terms, he exhibited *Musique aux Tuileries* at Martinet's gallery in 1863, a painting smaller and less precise in execution, in which a crowd is strung out across the whole canvas, without any focal point or centre of attention. The different type of work he showed in smaller exhibitions is most evident in the one-man show mounted in April 1880 at the offices of the magazine *La Vie moderne*, while *Chez le père Lathuille* and *Portrait de M. Antonin Proust* were on view at the Salon. Here he showed primarily scenes of modern urban entertainment (which was also a prime subject in the pages of *La Vie moderne*), including two café scenes, *Café-concert* and *Coin de café-concert*, which are in the present exhibition (Figs.46 and 54, Col.ills.5, 6).[37] The difference is very evident between their vivid, broken touch and multi-focus composition and the larger, more tightly worked *Un bar aux Folies-Bergère* (Fig.104, Col.ill.9), the only scene of popular entertainment Manet ever showed at the Salon, in which the figure of the barmaid, for all the ambiguities that surround it, is the iconic core of the composition.

However, the discussion of Manet's paintings does not belong only within the confines of the Salon. Salon painting was his prime medium, but the subject of his paintings was modern man's experience of the world around him; his sustained campaign of subversion against the conventions of Salon painting was his means of realising the aim he declared in 1867, to 'render his own impression'.[38] All of his friends spoke of his receptiveness to the scenes he saw around him and his alertness to possible pictorial effects. The surviving accounts of the genesis of many of his major pictures – among them *Le bain* and *Le balcon* – state that effects seen in passing, out of doors, were their initial stimulus.[39]

But what was the nature of his engagement with the modern world, and how can we gain access to it? Even the accounts of his friends seem contradictory, Zola seemingly demoting the significance of his subject matter in his 1867 article, while Mallarmé in 1876 stressed the modernity of the paintings, in theme and treatment. Zola's insistence that Manet rejected 'ideas' in favour of 'beautiful *taches*' does certainly contradict allegorical interpretations of his meanings, but it does not necessarily imply that Manet attributed no significance beyond the *tache* of colour to the modern scenes he chose to paint. Zola's case may in part have been an attempt to defuse the outcry which *Olympia* had aroused in 1865; but the wider purpose of his argument was to stress Manet's rejection of academic conventions and hierarchies of significance which placed the ideal, and 'ideas', above the real world. Writing in a different political framework and critical climate nine years later, Mallarmé could insist far more positively on the modernity of the paintings, presenting them not only as the rejection of academic artifice and convention, but also as expressions of 'the sentiment of their time', 'intransigent, which in political language means radical and democratic'.[40]

Mallarmé developed his argument from Manet's rejection of composition, be-cause 'the grouping of modern persons does not suggest it', and from his cultivation of the cut-off figure, to a remarkable passage in which he characterised the 'radical and democratic' implications of the art of Manet and his friends:

> At that critical hour for the human race when nature desires to work for herself, she requires certain lovers of hers – new and impersonal men placed directly in communion with the sentiment of their time – to loose the restraint of education, to let hand an eye do what they will, and thus, through them, reveal herself. For the mere pleasure of doing so? Certainly not, but to express herself, calm, naked, habitual, to those newcomers of tomorrow, of which each one will consent to be an unknown unit in the mighty numbers of an universal suffrage, and to place in their power a newer and more succinct means of observing her.[41]

But can Manet's paintings themselves sustain such a reading? Here we must turn again to what he rejected in contemporary 'education': the notions of form and fitness which treated painting according to the rules of comedy, and placed a higher value on a head than on a slipper; it was the 'arbitrariness' of his figures that baffled Castagnary, the 'pantheism' implied by his handling which disturbed Thoré.[42] These responses recognise that, in some deep-seated way, Manet's paintings challenged hallowed assumptions about human values and human relationships, about the centrality of the human interest and about the presentation of clear-cut hierarchies of significance and an orderly, comprehensible interplay between the participants. Manet's paintings presented a world which could not readily be decoded according to then-dominant systems of values. Viewed as they were by most critics in the 1860s solely within the canons of artistic judgement, they seemed merely crude and incompetent, but Thoré and Castagnary sensed that they raised wider questions; Castagnary's insistence that the painting should be self-contained like a comedy suggests that he felt that Manet's canvases threatened to break through the conventional confines of art, while Thoré's 'pantheism' relates their forms more directly to issues of fundamental belief. It is here that Mallarmé's eloquent account of the cut-off composition, a device which explicitly enshrines the idea that the painter has simply fixed on a fragment amid the crowd, presents the positive justification for these ruptures of conventional systems of coherence, as an image of the real, lived, world.

Such changing images of the 'real world' relate in part to actual changes in the modern environment: new forms of travel, notably the railway; the break-down of the traditional *quartiers* in Paris,[43] and the overall growth of the great industrial metropolis. But it is essential here to stress not just the physical changes, but the ways in which they were experienced – the fragmentary glimpses from the window of a train, and the break-down in the modern city of traditional ways of classifying and ordering man's surroundings. Recent commentators have noted a gradual change from mid- to late nineteenth century in the ways in which the crowd was characterised in writing, from a multifarious assembly whose varied ingredients can still be identified (Manet's 1862 *Le ballon* lithograph can be analysed in these terms) to an anonymous mass whose whole transcends the individuals who make it up. It is this latter crowd whose forms can be viewed cut by the picture frame, whose gestures can be presented out of context, with no indication of their purpose and meaning; of all Manet's paintings for the Salon, *Bal masqué à l'Opéra*, rejected by the jury in 1874, presents such a crowd most directly, with its left margin framed by the figure of Polichinelle, his right hand raised in a seemingly animated, yet illegible, gesture.[44]

However, we must not simply treat devices like these as pictorial or verbal strategies designed to reveal the 'real' world; their structures are value-laden, in what they select, what they highlight, and what relationships they construct. The bourgeois genre scenes of Stevens, Toulmouche, de Jonghe and their ilk are normative, not neutral: they formulate bourgeois ideology, rather than merely reflecting it, in their depictions of young women's pastimes, of courtship, of motherhood.

Manet's pictures transgressed these values in two ways: the relationships within them were not safely confined within the frame, and thus involved the unknown and the potentially dislocating; and, increasingly in his paintings of the 1870s, the status of the figures in them was ambivalent. Classification is a form of social control; readily identifiable categories can straightforwardly be located within systems of values. But these categories were coming under increasing strain in Paris in these years, particularly in questions of class and of sexual morality: in the status of the bourgeoisie, in the differentiation between the *monde* and the *demi-monde*, and in the margins of 'clandestine prostitution'.[45] The subjects of virtually all Manet's major paintings from the early 1870s on, apart from portraits, lay on these ambiguous borderlines, and their formal structures heightened these ambiguities, by denying the viewer the wherewithal to read and classify.

More than any other picture, *Un bar aux Folies-Bergère* (Fig.104, Col.ill.9) encapsulates these ambiguities, not only in the incompatibility of image with reflection, but also in the status of the barmaid. It has recently been proposed that she was a prostitute, but so precise a reading seems mistaken. Women who were explicitly prostitutes certainly plied their trade in the foyers and galleries of the Folies-Bergère, but the status of the barmaids was different: they probably belonged to the uncertain margins of clandestine prostitution, working first and foremost as barmaids, but potentially sexually available.[46] We cannot separate the uncertainty of the barmaid's status from the uncertainty of the relationship between the viewer and her images in the painting, which vacillates between the apparent intimacy in the reflection and the physical and psychic distance evoked by the figure who faces us out of the picture. Manet's achievement here is to give visual form to this range of uncertainties, about her status in society and about the nature of her relationship to her clients; and her gaze, turned out into our space, implicates us inextricably in these uncertainties – it is impossible to view this image as a self-contained world, confined within the frame.

In Manet's art, no communication is transparent, no values absolute; life, as he presented it, could not readily be decoded. For his opponents, his paintings were an attack on established hierarchies of art and on the values they upheld, but for his supporters they represented the reinstatement of nature and immediate experience in the place of artifice.

The appearance of the paintings was designed to heighten this sense of immediacy, but their effect was achieved only after Manet had taken the greatest pains, as Théodore de Banville testified when writing about *Le bon bock* in 1873: 'It is truth itself, seized, or so one would believe, in a moment of luminous inspiration, if one did not know how much knowledge and study are needed to make works which seem to blossom so spontaneously and effortlessly.'[47] Throughout his working process, Manet eschewed stock academic practice, in which the preliminary studies and the preparation of the canvas itself were so comprehensive that the execution of the finished work was an essentially mechanical procedure. As the present exhibition eloquently testifies, his working methods enshrined a sort of indeterminacy; as Zola wrote in 1884, 'when he began a painting, he would never be able to say how it would turn out'.[48] He treated the surface of the final canvas itself as a sort of workshop, using his first ideas and notations as the triggers for revisions and, on occasion, wholesale recompositions of his pictures. X-ray examination goes a long way to revealing this 'hidden face of Manet', but we must assume that much more was actually erased from the canvas before reworking. J.-É. Blanche wrote that Manet 'laboured greatly on the paintings he sent to the Salon, yet they looked like sketches', and that he 'rubbed out and repainted incessantly'; for his portrait of Antonin Proust, he apparently started seven or eight canvases before achieving the successful version 'at one go'.[49] It was, of course, the accumulated experience of the previous versions that allowed him to realise the final one so immediately, and to give it the air of freshness he sought. Yet, despite the apparent spontaneity of his final surfaces, they were far from being just rapid sketches from nature. Georges Jeanniot watched him at work on *Un bar aux Folies-Bergère*: 'Although he worked from the model, he did not copy nature at all closely; I noted his masterly simplifications. . . . Everything was abbreviated; the tones were made lighter, the colours brighter; the values were more closely related to each other, the tones more contrasting. . . .' Manet, he reported, used to say things like: ' "Concision in art is a necessity, and also a matter of good style; the concise man makes you think, the verbose man is a bore; always work towards concision." '[50] As in *Un bar aux Folies-Bergère*, his starting point was always rooted in visual experience of the world around him, but the pictorial process distilled and transformed this raw material, so that the final results enshrined the ambivalence and incoherence of his chosen subjects in coherent pictorial form.

This last phrase, though, reveals the paradox of Manet's legacy. The forms which so vigorously challenged contemporary values were readily assimilated into the formalist concerns of the emerging modern movement, which emphasised the surface qualities of the picture at the expense of its social meanings. In retrospect, Zola's 1867 essay, with its emphasis on the *tache* of colour, may have sanctioned this when read outside its original context, but an analysis of this process of assimilation would be the subject for another essay. However, the present-day historian cannot ignore this legacy; we may now seek to present Manet's production within a fuller historical context, but we cannot detach ourselves from our own viewpoint.

The current reaction against modernism defines itself as the antithesis of the values it rejects: cultural pluralism and ambivalence have replaced the clear-cut value judgements and authoritative readings of the modernist tradition. Though we question the modernist canon, our questioning is inevitably couched within its terms of reference. We should not deny that this presentation of our own position bears a close resemblance to the context I have here proposed for Manet; in some way the re-presentation of the past is inevitably a presentation of the present.[51] But we must use this awareness positively, seeking to refine our understanding of the past by defining as closely as possible both the similarities and the differences between present and past debates.

Notes

I am most grateful to four people for their valuable comments on this essay, to Juliet Wilson Bareau and Neil MacGregor, instigators and organisers of the present exhibition, and to Kathleen Adler and Jill House. The following abbreviations are used in the footnotes: TABARANT [1947]: A. TABARANT: *Manet et ses œuvres*, Paris [1947]; HAMILTON [1954]: G. H. HAMILTON: *Manet and his Critics*, New Haven [1954]; CLARK [1985]: T. J. CLARK: *The Painting of Modern Life, Paris in the Art of Manet and his Followers*, London [1985].

1 For sources, cf. notably M. FRIED: 'Manet's Sources', *Artforum* [March 1969] and T. REFF: ' "Manet's Sources": a critical evaluation', *Artforum* [September 1969]; for allegorical interpretations, G. MAUNER: *Manet Peintre-Philosophe, A study of the Painter's Themes*, University Park and London [1975]; for analysis of social context (from two very different viewpoints), T. REFF: *Manet and Modern Paris*, Washington and Chicago [1982], and CLARK [1985].

2 'Sincérité', cf. Manet's 'Motifs d'une exposition particulière', published as a preface to the catalogue of his 1867 one-man exhibition (quoted in P. COURTHION (ed.): *Manet raconté par lui-même et par ses amis*, Geneva [1953], I, pp.134–36). Camille de Sainte-Croix quoted Manet's comment: '*On n'est pas un artiste quand on n'est pas un primitif*' (quoted in MAUNER, *op. cit.* at note 1 above, p.1, note 1).

3 E. ZOLA: 'Édouard Manet', *Revue de XIXe siècle* [1st January 1867], quoted in *Mon Salon, Manet, Ecrits sur l'art*, Paris [1970], pp.95–96, 101; C. BAUDELAIRE: *Salon de 1846*, and 'Le Peintre de la vie moderne', *Le Figaro* [26th, 29th November, 3rd December 1863], quoted in *Ecrits sur l'art*, Paris [1971], I, pp.144, 162, 250; II, p.144; CHAMPFLEURY: *Histoire de l'imagerie populaire*, Paris [1869, 1886 edition], p.XLVII.

4 Letter from Baudelaire to Arsène Houssaye, December 1861, in C. BAUDELAIRE: *Correspondance générale*, Paris [1948], IV, p.34.

5 ZOLA, *loc. cit.* at note 3 above, pp.95, 101: '*ce peintre assurément peint d'une façon toute naïve et toute recueillie . . . avec quelle naïveté il se place devant la nature*'; BAUDELAIRE, *op. cit.* at note 3 above, I, p.162 (Salon de 1846): '*Il faut entendre par la naïveté du génie la science du métier combinée avec le gnôti seauton, mais la science modeste laissant le beau rôle au tempérament*'; II, p.144 (published 1863): '*. . . le génie n'est que l'enfance retrouvée à volonté, l'enfance douée maintenant, pour s'exprimer, d'organes virils et de l'esprit analytique qui lui permet d'ordonner la somme de matériaux involontairement amassée*'; CHAMPFLEURY, *op. cit.* at note 3 above: '*On n'apprend pas la naïveté. La naïveté vient du coeur, non du cerveau*'.

6 S. MALLARMÉ: 'The Impressionists and Edouard Manet', *Art Monthly Review* [September 1876], quoted in C. P. BARBIER (ed.): *Documents Stéphane Mallarmé*, Paris [1968], I, pp.69ff., 76; the original French text of Mallarmé's essay does not survive; it exists only in English, as published in 1876.

7 MANET, 'Motifs . . .', cited at note 2 above: *'L'artiste ne dit pas aujourd'hui: venez voir des œuvres sans défauts, mais: venez voir des œuvres sincères. C'est l'effet de la sincérité de donner aux œuvres un caractère qui les fait ressembler à une protestation, alors que le peintre n'a songé qu'à rendre son impression. M. Manet n'a jamais voulu protester. C'est contre lui, qui ne s'y attendait pas, qu'on a protesté au contraire, parce qu'il y a un enseignement traditionnel de formes, de moyens, d'aspects de peinture, et que ceux qui ont été élevés dans de tels principes n'en admettent plus d'autres. . . . En dehors de leurs formules rien ne peut valoir, et ils se font non seulement critiques, mais adversaires actifs.'*

8 A. PROUST: 'L'Art d'Édouard Manet', *Le Studio* [15th January 1901], p.76: *'Les imbéciles! ils n'ont cessé de me dire que j'étais inégal: ils ne pourraient rien dire de plus élogieux. Cela a toujours été mon ambition de ne pas demeurer égal à moi-même, de ne pas refaire, le lendemain, ce que j'avais fait la veille, de m'inspirer constamment d'un aspect nouveau, de chercher à faire entendre une note nouvelle.'* Credence is lent to this passage in Proust's reminiscences of Manet by a comment in his review of the 1882 Salon (A. PROUST: 'Le Salon de 1882 [1er article]', *Gazette des Beaux-Arts* [June 1882], p.547): *'. . . en artiste convaincu, il ne se croit pas autorisé à refaire la chose qui a réussi et pense qu'il faut sans cesse ajouter les tentatives aux tentatives déjà faites.'*

9 HAMILTON [1954], CLARK [1985]; there are also extensive, but abbreviated, extracts from the criticism in TABARANT [1947]. One example of Hamilton's tendency to impose subsequent preoccupations on Manet's early critics is highlighted by CLARK (pp.290–91, note 75, and p.295, note 130); CLARK rightly insists that Gonzague Privat's 1865 comment, that *'le public . . . ne comprend rien du tout à cet art trop abstrait pour son intelligence'*, must be understood in the context of contemporary discussions of the 'abstract' in the depiction of the nude, and not viewed as a pioneering assertion of the primacy of 'colours and forms' in Manet's art. For a comprehensive bibliography of Salon criticism during the Second Empire, cf. C. PARSONS and M. WARD: *Bibliography of Salon Criticism in Second Empire Paris*, Cambridge, forthcoming [1986].

10 For reiterated stereotypes, cf. note 11; most noteworthy among the critics who moved gradually from criticism to support of Manet's art after 1870 were perhaps Ernest Chesneau, Jules Castagnary and Albert Wolff.

11 L. LEROY, in *Le Charivari* [4th June 1868], quoted in HAMILTON [1954], p.127: *'A la fin de la séance d'hier, j'ai oublié de mentionner une demi-douzaine de points sur lesquels mon manque de croyances est complet: je nie la forme, je nie la ligne, je nie la composition, je nie le sens commun, je nie . . . je nie la vertu . . . je nie la distinction . . . je nie tout le monde . . . je nie la poésie . . . je nie la vérité . . . je nie la civilisation. . . .'* These last denials are responses to comments made by other pictures in this strange symposium. The interjections from the Zola portrait might almost have been made by the parrot in Manet's other exhibit in the same Salon, his *Femme au perroquet*. For late examples of these critical stereotypes about Manet, cf. the comments by Roger Ballu and Bertall about Manet's 1880 exhibits, quoted in HAMILTON [1954], pp.230, 235.

12 THORÉ, in *L'Indépendance belge* [29th June 1868], reprinted in T. THORÉ: *Salons de W. Bürger, 1861 à 1868*, Paris [1870], II, pp.531–32: *'Quand il a fait sur sa toile ''la tache de couleur'' que font sur la nature ambiante un personnage ou un objet, il se tient quitte. Ne lui en demandez pas plus long, – pour le moment. Mais il se débrouillera plus tard, quand il songera à donner leur valeur relative aux parties essentielles des êtres. Son vice actuel est une sorte de panthéisme qui n'estime pas plus une tête qu'une pantoufle; qui parfois accorde même plus d'importance à un bouquet de fleurs qu'à la physionomie d'une femme . . . qui peint tout presque uniformément, les meubles, les tapis, les livres, les costumes, les chairs, les accents du visage.'* For Thoré's similar comment in 1863, cf. *ibid.*, I, pp.424–25; MANTZ, in *L'Illustration* [6th June 1868], quoted by HAMILTON [1954], p.121; J. CASTAGNARY, in *Le Siècle* [29th May 1875], quoted by HAMILTON [1954], p.193.

13 For instance, cf. REDON, in *La Gironde* [9th June 1868], quoted by HAMILTON [1954], p.129; CASTAGNARY [1875], as cited at note 12 above; A. WOLFF, in *Le Figaro* [17th April 1876], quoted by TABARANT [1947], p.283; BAIGNÈRES, in *Gazette des Beaux-Arts* [1st June 1879], quoted by HAMILTON [1954], p.214.

14 CHAUMELIN, in *L'Indépendance belge* [29th June 1869], quoted by TABARANT [1947], p.161: *'Ses deux tableaux . . . ont fortement scandalisé les amateurs de peinture proprette, nette, sentimentale et bourgeoise. . . . Pas d'expression, pas de sentiment, pas de composition.'* DURANTY, in *Paris-Journal* [5th May 1870], quoted by TABARANT [1947], pp.176–77: *'A la peinture raffinée, ficelle, M. Manet oppose une naïveté systématique, le dédain de tous les moyens séducteurs. C'est sur un fond gris sombre, ardoisé, qu'il installe ses personnages, comme s'il protestait puritainement contre ces mobiliers de bric-à-brac que la grande et la petite toulmoucherie, et les nature-mortiers, entassent de peur de passer pour pauvres.'*

15 JUNIUS, in *Le Gaulois* [25th April 1875], quoted by TABARANT [1947], p.286: *'. . . sa haine excentrique du banal et du convenu'*; A. WOLFF, in *Figaro-Salon* [1st May 1882], quoted by TABARANT [1947], p.439: *'sa haine de la peinture frisée et pommandée le fait souvent dépasser le but'*.

16 LAGRANGE, in *Gazette des Beaux-Arts* [1st July 1861], quoted exh. cat. Paris, Grand Palais, *Manet* [1983], p.50: *'Mais quel fléau dans la société qu'un peintre réaliste! Pour lui, rien de sacré: M. Manet foule aux pieds des affections plus saintes encore.'*

17 T. GAUTIER, in *L'Illustration* [15th May 1869], p.311, quoted by HAMILTON [1954], p.134: *'Mais pourquoi ces armes sur la table? Est-ce le déjeuner qui suit ou qui précède un duel? Nous ne savons'* (in fact the armour is on a chair); MANTZ, in *Gazette des Beaux-Arts* [July 1869], p.13, quoted by HAMILTON [1954], pp.135–36: *'On ne sait bien ce que ces honnêtes personnes font à leur balcon, et les critiques allemands, curieux du sens philosophique des choses, seraient ici fort en peine pour comprendre et pour expliquer.'*

18 J. CASTAGNARY, in *Le Siècle* [11th June 1869], reprinted in J. CASTAGNARY: *Salons (1857–1879)*, Paris [1892], pp.364–65: *'En regardant ce Déjeuner . . . je vois, sur une table où le café est servi, un citron à moitié pelé et des huîtres fraîches. Ces objets ne marchent guère ensemble. Pourquoi les avoir mis? . . . De même que M. Manet assemble, pour le seul plaisir de frapper les yeux, des natures mortes qui devraient s'exclure; de même, il distribue ses personnages au hasard, sans que rien de nécessaire et de forcé ne commande leur composition. De là l'incertitude, et souvent l'obscurité dans la pensée. Que fait ce jeune homme du Déjeuner, qui est assis au premier plan et qui semble regarder le public? . . . où est-il? Dans la salle à manger? Alors, ayant le dos à la table, il a le mur entre lui et nous, et sa position ne s'explique plus. Sur ce Balcon j'aperçois deux femmes, dont une toute jeune. Sont-ce les deux soeurs? Est-ce la mère et la fille? Je ne sais. Et puis, l'une est assise et semble s'être placée uniquement pour jouir du spectacle de la rue; l'autre se gante comme si elle allait sortir. Cette attitude contradictoire me déroute. . . . Mais le sentiment des fonctions, mais le sentiment de la convenance sont choses indispensables. Ni l'écrivain, ni le peintre ne les peuvent supprimer. Comme les personnages dans une comédie, il faut que dans un tableau chaque figure soit à son plan, remplisse son rôle et concoure ainsi à l'expression de l'idée générale. Rien d'arbitraire et rien de superflu, telle est la loi du toute composition artistique.'*

19 DUVERGIER DE HAURANNE, in *Revue des deux mondes* [1st June 1874], quoted by HAMILTON [1954], p.179: *'Est-ce un portrait à deux personnages ou un tableau de style que le Chemin de fer de M. Manet . . . ? Les informations nous manquent pour résoudre ce problème; nous hésitons d'autant plus qu'en ce qui concerne la jeune fille, ce serait tout au moins un portrait vu de dos.'* For the mirror in *Un bar*, cf. the comments by Comte, du Seigneur, Bergerat and Stop, quoted in CLARK [1985], pp.311–13, notes 68, 71, 72, 75.

20 ZOLA, *op. cit.* at note 3 above, pp.100–01; MANTZ, *loc. cit.* at note 17 above: *'Admettons qu'il s'agit d'une combinaison de couleurs'*; CASTAGNARY, *loc. cit.* at note 18 above: *'C'est parce que M. Manet a au plus haut point le sentiment de la tache colorante.'*

21 E. CHESNEAU, in *Annuaire illustré des Beaux-Arts: 1882*, quoted by CLARK [1985], p.313 note 82: *'Ce mérite est dans la juste vision des choses, de leur coloration, de leur vibration lumineuse, de leur apparence ondoyante et passante si fugitive, si rapide.'*

22 MARC DE MONTIFAUD, in *L'Artiste* [1st June 1873], p.282, quoted by HAMILTON [1954], p.170: *'Ne demandez pas au tableau de composition de règles préétablies, l'auteur ne les connaît pas ou ne veut pas les connaître, mais seulement la note franche et dominante que tout objet prend dans la nature. M. Manet ne cherche point l'âme de la physionomie, mais plutôt son enveloppe.'*

23 MALLARMÉ, *loc. cit.* at note 6 above, pp.76–77.

24 A. PROUST: 'Édouard Manet (Souvenirs)', *Revue blanche* [1st March 1897], pp.202–03: *'Alfred Stevens avait peint un tableau représentant une femme qui écartait un rideau. Au pied de ce rideau était un plumeau qui jouait là le rôle de l'adjectif inutile dans une belle phrase de prose ou de la cheville dans un vers bien venu. ''Tout s'explique'', avait dit Manet, ''cette femme attend le valet de chambre''.'* The picture in question can be identified as *La visite matinale*, formerly Coll. A. Sarens, sold Brussels, Galerie Royale, 7th December 1923, lot 51.

25 A. PROUST: 'Édouard Manet (Souvenirs)', *Revue blanche* [1st February 1897], especially pp.126–28, 132–33. Proust's reminiscences of Manet's youth have aroused considerable scepticism, because he seems to have known Manet less well than he implies, and because the tone of his account is so deeply impregnated by knowledge of the rôle that Manet was later to play in the battles around 'naturalism' and 'impressionism'; however, the nature of Manet's first Salon submission, *Le buveur d'absinthe*, rejected in 1859, at least confirms that from the start of his public career he was concerned with finding an anti-academic treatment for subjects from everyday life.

26 Examples of alternative 'sources' proposed for a single figure are the Le Nain figures and the Hellenistic 'Chrysippos' statuette for the figure of the musician in *Le vieux musicien* (DE LEIRIS: 'Manet, Guéroult and Chrysippos', *Art Bulletin* 46 [1964], pp.401–04; FRIED, *loc. cit.* at note 1 above, pp.30–32; REFF [1969], *loc. cit.* at note 1 above, p.43), and the figures from Watteau and Raphael compared to the background bather in *Le bain* (*Le déjeuner sur l'herbe*; FRIED, *loc. cit.* at note 1 above, p.40; REFF [1969], *loc. cit.* at note 1 above, p.46).

27 CLARK [1985], pp.119–31 contains a particularly valuable discussion of the relationship between *Olympia* and the conventions of the Salon nude.

28 Thoré's discussion of *Le bain* is helpful in indicating the problems which the picture presented to its original viewers (THORÉ, *op. cit.* at note 12 above, I, p.425): *'Le Bain est d'un goût très-risqué. . . . La femme nue n'est pas de belle forme, malheureusement, et on n'imaginerait rien de plus laid que le monsieur étendu près d'elle et qui n'a pas même eu l'idée d'ôter, en plein air, son horrible chapeau en bourrelet. C'est ce contraste d'un animal si antipathique au caractère d'une scène champêtre, avec cette baigneuse sans voiles, qui est choquant. Je ne devine pas ce qui a pu faire choisir à un artiste intelligent et distingué une composition si absurde, que l'élégance et le charme des personnages eussent peut-être justifiée.'*

29 J. RICHARDSON: *Manet*, London [1958], p.13; for more recent discussions, cf. FRIED, REFF [1969] and REFF [1982], *loc. cit.* at note 1 above; DE LEIRIS, *loc. cit.* at note 26 above, and M. R. BROWN: 'Manet's *Old Musician*: Portrait of a Gypsy and Naturalist Allegory', *Studies in the History of Art*, 8, National Gallery of Art, Washington, D.C. [1978], with bibliography p.77 note 3.

30 CHAMPFLEURY: 'Nouvelles recherches sur la vie et l'œuvre des frères Le Nain', *Gazette des Beaux-Arts* 8 [1860], p.180: *'Leur façon de composer est anti-académique; elle échappe aux plus simples lois, ils ne s'inquiètent pas de grouper leurs personnages. . . . Ils ont cherché la réalité jusque dans cette inhabileté à placer des figures isolées au milieu de la toile; par là ils sont les pères des tentatives actuelles, et leur réputation ne peut que s'accroître.'* MAUNER, *op. cit.* at note 1 above, p.65, quotes this passage, but I am unable to accept his ensuing allegorical interpretation of *Le vieux musicien*.

31 A. COFFIN HANSON first noted the Schlesinger, but quite rightly noted that its 'presentation, both informative and anecdotal, is completely opposite in spirit' to Manet's canvas: *Manet and the Modern Tradition*, New Haven and London [1977], p.63; however, REFF has since presented it quite uncritically as 'the latest and perhaps least expected' source to be discovered for *Le vieux musicien* (REFF [1982], *loc. cit.* at note 1 above, p.188).

32 For fashionable women with pets, cf. Alfred Stevens, *Le départ pour le promenade*, 1859 (Philadelphia Museum of Art, repr. exh. cat. Ann Arbor, University of Michigan Museum of Art, *Alfred Stevens*, 1977, No.4); during the 1860s, Gustave de Jonghe made a speciality of pictures of fashionably dressed women behaving flirtatiously with parrots on perches.

33 For the *Exécution*, cf. pp.48–64 of this issue, and the dossier of documents in exh. cat. Paris/New York [1983], pp.529–31.

34 Cf. above, p.7 and note 14.

35 The oddities in *En bateau* are given an unequivocally formalist interpretation in exh. cat. Paris/New York [1983], p.359, but this ignores the expectations of thematic coherence and legibility which the painting's original viewers would have brought to it. I am indebted to Theo Cowdell for detailed analysis of the oddities of this boat.

36 I am grateful to Robert Herbert for pointing out to me that the man in *Chez le père Lathuille* has no chair. X-rays of the painting, shown me by Juliet Bareau, show that originally the waiter was looking at the couple, as in Tissot's canvas; Manet's decision to turn his gaze towards the viewer makes the scene less legible and less self-contained.

37 Besides these two café scenes, Manet showed the following oils at *La Vie moderne*: *Portrait de M.D. . . . avocat*; *La prune*; *Le peintre Claude Monet dans son atelier*; *Un skating*; *Portrait de M.B. . . .*; *Devant la glace*; *Fleurs (étude décorative)*; *La lecture* (D. ROUART and D. WILDENSTEIN: *Édouard Manet, catalogue raisonné*, Lausanne and Paris [1975], Nos.294, 282, 219, 260, 326, 264, 247, 136); in addition he showed fifteen pastels – a type of work he never submitted to the Salon. Manet's willingness to put these more informal works before the public in a small exhibition such as this would have made his refusal to participate in the impressionists' group exhibitions all the more pointed, since these exhibitions were conceived as outlets for just such works, of a type unsuitable for the Salon.

38 MANET, 'Motifs . . .', cited at note 2 above.

39 For *Le bain*, cf. A. PROUST: 'Édouard Manet (Souvenirs)', *Revue blanche* [15th February 1897], p.171; for *Le balcon*, cf. E. MOREAU-NÉLATON: *Manet raconté par lui-même*, Paris [1926], I, p.105.

40 ZOLA, *loc. cit.* at note 3 above, pp.100–01; MALLARMÉ, *loc. cit.* at note 6 above, pp.69–70, 84. It is perhaps noteworthy that Mallarmé's radical interpretation was only published in England.

41 MALLARMÉ, *loc. cit.* at note 6 above, pp.76–77, 84–85; the oddities of the surviving English version of Mallarmé's essay become more marked in its latter parts, such as the passage quoted here, and notably in its conclusion.

42 CASTAGNARY, *loc. cit.* at note 18 above; THORÉ, *loc. cit.* at note 12 above.

43 On the break-down of the *quartiers*, cf. CLARK [1985], pp.50–60.

44 On *Bal masqué à l'Opéra*, cf. L. NOCHLIN: 'A Thoroughly Modern Masked Ball', *Art in America* [November 1983]; changing perceptions of the crowd in the literature of the later nineteenth century are discussed in S. BARROWS: *Distorting Mirrors, Visions of the Crowd in Late Nineteenth-Century France*, New Haven and London [1981], and R. WILLIAMS: *The Country and the City*, London [1973]; for discussion of Renoir's inability to depict the 'new' crowd, cf. J. HOUSE: 'Renoir and the Earthly Paradise', *Oxford Art Journal*, 8.2 [1986].

45 Like all other recent accounts of prostitution in Paris, I am indebted here to A. CORBIN: *Les Filles de noce*, Paris [1978]; for discussions related to Manet, cf. CLARK [1985]; T. A. GRONBERG: 'Femmes de brasserie', *Art History* [September 1984]; and H. CLAYSON: 'Avant-Garde and *Pompier* Images of 19th Century Prostitution: The Matter of Modernism, Modernity and Social Ideology', in B. BUCHLOH, S. GUILBAUT, D. SOLKIN (eds.): *Modernism and Modernity*, Halifax, Nova Scotia [1983].

46 For contemporary evocations of the Folies-Bergère, cf. J.-K. HUYSMANS: 'Les Folies-Bergère en 1879', in *Croquis parisiens*, Paris [1880], and the descriptions of the place as a scenario for the fictional action in G. DE MAUPASSANT: *Bel-Ami*, Paris [1885].

47 T. DE BANVILLE, in *Le National* [15th May 1873], quoted by TABARANT [1947], p.206: *'C'est la vérité même, saisie, à ce qu'on croirait, dans une heure d'improvisation lumineuse, si l'on ne savait ce qu'il faut de science et d'étude pour faire des œuvres qui semblent ainsi être écloses spontanément et sans effort.'*

48 E. ZOLA: 'Édouard Manet' [1884], in ZOLA, *op. cit.* at note 3 above, p.362: *'En commençant un tableau, jamais il n'aurait pu dire comment ce tableau viendrait.'*

49 J.-É. BLANCHE: *Manet*, Paris [1924], pp.30, 51: *'Quoiqu'il peinât fort sur ses "envois" de Salon, on dirait pourtant des esquisses, tant la fraîcheur de ton (de la première heure d'ébauche) est peu ternie par le travail.' 'Il grattait, recommençait sans répit.'* A. PROUST: 'Édouard Manet (Souvenirs)', *Revue blanche* [15th March 1897], p.308: *'Après avoir usé sept ou huit toiles, le portrait venait d'un seul coup.'* Proust's account seems to imply that Manet began each time on a fresh canvas, but he may well have wiped out before starting afresh on the same canvas.

50 G. JEANNIOT: 'En Souvenir de Manet', *La Grande Revue* [10th August 1907], p.853; *'Manet, bien que peignant ses tableaux d'après le modèle, ne copiait pas du tout la nature; je me rendis compte de ses magistrales simplifications. . . . Tout était abrégé; les tons étaient plus clairs, les couleurs plus vives, les valeurs plus voisines, les tons plus différents. . . . La concision en art est une nécessité et une élégance; l'homme concis fait réfléchir, l'homme verbeux ennuie; modifiez-vous toujours dans le sens de la concision.'*

51 For a salutary reminder of how far twentieth-century interpretations of Manet have been reflections of current preoccupations, cf. D. CARRIER: 'Manet and his interpreters', *Art History* [September 1985].

In memory of Tomás Harris
Juan Corradini

Introduction
by Juliet Wilson Bareau

Fig.17a. *Le gamin*. 1861–62. Etching. 20.9 by 14.8 cm. Signed u.l. *éd. Manet*. (Bibliothèque Nationale, Cabinet des Estampes, Paris.)

Fig.17b. *Le gamin*. c.1872. Lithograph. 28.9 by 22.8 cm. Signed u.l. *Manet*. (Bibliothèque Nationale, Cabinet des Estampes, Paris.)

This study began as an attempt to solve particular problems relating to Manet's paintings, prints and drawings. It has ended by demonstrating that Manet's artistic enterprise was a formidably intelligent one, with a quite remarkable unity and coherence. Any disjointedness, any apparently ragged edges, are due largely to our lack of understanding of the ways in which he developed his paintings. If one looks for them, the cut and ragged edges of his canvases will tell us, quite literally, about the reshaping of pictures or their joining with other canvases, while X-rays and the analysis of pigments can reveal painting that lies hidden beneath the surface.

This is not news. Historians like Theodore Reff, Anne Coffin Hanson, Jean Harris and Charles Stuckey have shown the kind of information that X-rays and the patient reconstruction of lost canvases can provide. But although fascinating individual results have been reported, there has been no systematic attempt to apply these methods to Manet's work as a whole.

By a happy chance, which I owe to Michel Melot and Françoise Cachin, I became involved, first as a Manet 'print specialist' and then, with Charles Stuckey, as one of the general coordinators, in the great 1983 Manet retrospective held in Paris and New York. As we scrambled then to digest and classify the enormous amount of old and new information on Manet's art before the catalogue deadlines, we could see the areas that required investigation. And when the exhibition went up on the walls in Paris, the questions became more clearly defined. At the Metropolitan Museum in New York, it was possible, thanks to the cooperation of Gisela Helmkampf, to X-ray many pictures (a process already started, at Charles Stuckey's urging, when the exhibition plans got under way). After that, one thing led to another, as each new question resulted in physical examination of a work and led to further questions about the implications of that examination.

Although I had been impressed by previous publications of X-ray results and had looked with great interest at Juan Corradini's study of the *Nymphe surprise* (**15** and **16**, Figs.40 and 41), it is perhaps worth relating the event which made me feel that a print specialist could become involved in the discussion of Manet's paintings. Among the early pictures in the 1983 exhibition was the virtually unknown *Boy with a dog*. Manet reproduced this attractive work in an etching and a lithograph, but the two prints are not identical (Figs.17a and b). The etching, published in 1862, is rather different from the picture. The lithograph, published much later, in 1874 (together with Manet's *Guerre civile* lithograph, **41**, Fig.76), is identical with the oil painting. I had assumed, like everyone else, that the etching was a 'free' copy while the lithograph was a faithful transcription, probably based on a photograph of the painting. When the picture was unpacked and hung, it did not fit in with the other early works. It also showed signs of having been reworked. In New York, X-ray examination confirmed that the original, underlying painting was identical with the 1862 etching, while the 1874 lithograph reflected its final, repainted state and format.

A long apprenticeship with Goya's prints under Tomás Harris, and an intense study of the prints of Manet, thanks to Huguette Berès and François Lachenal, have produced a confirmed addict of 'states' – the often minutely different states that can be observed in proofs taken from a copperplate or lithographic stone in the course of work. Through X-rays, the 'states' of paintings can be studied in the same way, with the help of related prints and drawings.

At the time of the Paris–New York retrospective in 1983, other Manet exhibitions were held. In Washington, D.C., Theodore Reff's *Manet and Modern Paris* included the fascinating reconstruction of *Episode d'une course de taureaux*, the bullfight painting that Manet cut and largely destroyed after showing it at the Salon of 1864. And at the National Gallery in London, Michael Wilson mounted the exceptionally interesting *Manet at Work* exhibition, to which David Bomford and Ashok Roy contributed a brilliant analysis of the newly cleaned and X-rayed *Waitress* (**46**, Fig.82, Col.ill.5).

In that exhibition, the sketch for the *Execution of Maximilian* (**35**, Fig.69, Col.ill.10), from Copenhagen, caught my eye. Documents published by Antony Griffiths have confirmed that Manet intended to publish a lithograph when he presented his great painting at the Salon of 1869. It has always seemed puzzling that the lithograph (**34**, Fig.68) does not correspond with the composition of any of the three large paintings or the Copenhagen sketch. Since the sketch showed evident signs of having been reworked, permission was sought to have it X-rayed, and the underlying image proved to be extremely close to the lithographic design.

In the end, and with results still coming in as this study goes to press, it has been possible to attempt an analysis of three groups of works, which span the whole of Manet's career. The first explores the themes of the seated and reclining nude, which led up to two early masterpieces, the *Déjeuner sur l'herbe* and *Olympia*. The second is the series of works devoted to the *Execution of Maximilian*. And finally, an examination of all the café-concert pictures has led to a much clearer understanding of their development, from the dismembered *Reichshoffen* painting of c.1877 to Manet's final masterpiece, *Un bar aux Folies-Bergère*.

This intense activity at home and abroad was carried on thanks to the enthusiasm and support of colleagues in all the institutions concerned. The results were not always easy to interpret, and throughout this piece of research, I have relied very much on discussing new evidence and ideas and testing theories on friends and colleagues. I hope they did not find it quite as painful as the endless poses to which Manet subjected his models, but they have been in large part responsible for clarifying the new ideas and setting the material in perspective, when it threatened to get out of hand. Indeed, I was saved, with ultimate gallantry, from misconstruing my own deductions with regard to the final conclusion.

I owe an immense debt to Neil MacGregor, John House, Charles Stuckey, David Bomford, Lola Faillant-Dumas and Melanie Gifford. And Robert Bruce-Gardiner, in the Technology Department of the Courtauld Institute, played an essential rôle. He not only devoted many hours to the expert copying, cutting and joining of the X-ray films, on which so much of this research and the exhibition depend, but also discussed the material with patience, knowledge and understanding.

Because of the complexity or incompleteness of the material, some of the conclusions reached here are bound to be subject to revision. The evidence has been analysed as objectively as possible, with an eye for 'states' and constant reference to the documentary facts (such as the information provided by Léon Leenhoff's register of Manet's works and the annotated Lochard photographs). The results suggest that this kind of study should be applied to the rest of Manet's œuvre. Indeed, if it became an accepted part of museum practice and the art historical process, it could illuminate the whole of nineteenth-century painting. Only when the works themselves have revealed all they have to tell us about their actual making, can theory and speculation be projected from a sound basis in fact.

Hors d'Oeuvre

Quite early on in the investigation of paintings for this project, I saw the splendid still-life of *Le jambon* (**II**, Fig.19) at the Burrell Collection, Glasgow. It showed distinct signs of having been reworked and an X-ray was requested and duly made. Since the painting and its X-ray image (**I**, Fig.18) are an excellent demonstration of the results which physical examination of a canvas can provide, they serve here as an introduction, an *hors d'œuvre*, to the main text.

Le jambon was bought by Manet's friend, the lion-hunter Pertuiset, in 1882. He acquired many of the artist's late still-lifes, usually of fruit and flowers. These pictures are generally freshly and freely painted, with the bare, primed canvas often showing between the brushstrokes. The *Ham*, on the other hand, is richly and thickly painted; the bare canvas is nowhere visible; and surface cracks suggest that paint was applied over an incompletely dry layer (cracks being produced by different rates of drying in different layers). Cracking is particularly noticeable in the upper and lower right corners, and in the lower corner, an underlying shape suggests that Manet painted over something that once lay on the tablecloth. X-ray examination of the canvas was carried out, with unsuspected and interesting results.

When a painting is subjected to X-radiography, all its structural components – stretcher, canvas, ground and the paint itself – are recorded in depth, just like the layers of tissue and bone in the human body. Lead white is one of the most dense and X-radiographically opaque pigments and so, when used alone or mixed with other pigments, it produces sensitive and accurate readings. Since Manet, like most artists, mixed his paints with a lot of lead white, they usually provide a clear and readable image of the underlying layers, and this is true of the *Ham*. It can be seen from the X-ray films as well as from the positive photographic print made from them (Fig.18), that the ham sits unchanged while everything around it was altered by the artist.

The ham itself is painted in thin, translucent layers which suggest the bloom on the succulent piece of meat and the texture of the fat and rind. Since it remained unchanged, and was relatively thinly painted in pigments which contain very little lead white, the X-rays passed through it unhindered and it shows as a very dark shape. In the X-ray image, the ham is sitting on a dish whose farther rim lies below the edge of the table. In front of the dish lies the same knife, but to the right the round shape of a fruit or vegetable is clearly visible, its left edge almost touching the point of the knife. Manet painted out this object, and rearranged the folds in the tablecloth. He eliminated one rather bumpy fold which runs under the knife blade and disappears beneath the dish, repainting the tablecloth with two thin creases that run back in diverging diagonals, to the left of the dish and under the tip of the knife blade.

The X-ray image also shows an object or objects on the far side of the tablecloth, to the right. In the final painting, these objects have been eliminated and the right edge of the silver dish is raised so that its perspective is 'incorrect'. (It could never meet the rim of the dish which re-emerges behind the left edge of the ham.)

The lack of lead white or other X-ray opaque pigments in the paint over the

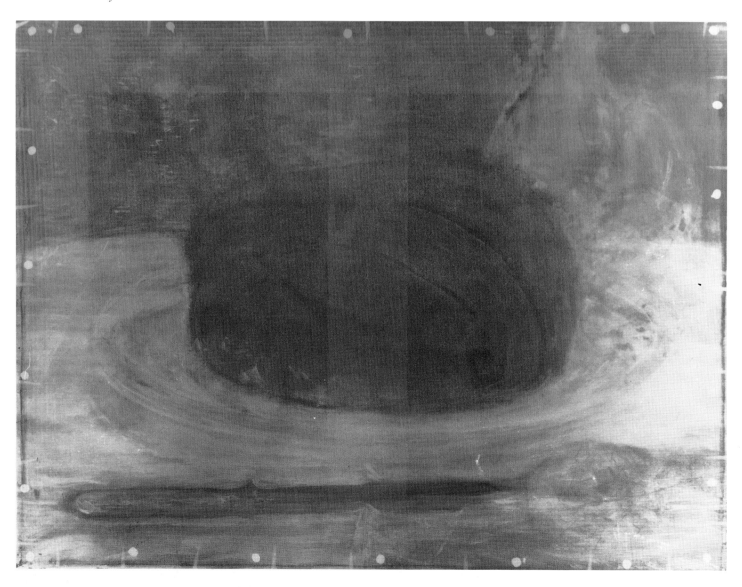

background (and the distracting X-ray image of the stretcher bars and tacks around the edges of the canvas), make it difficult to judge whether the richly patterned background was present in the original design. The present background, which covers the objects on the table, recalls the brocade or painted screen, with a crane, which appears in works of the 1870s (the pictures of *Nina* and *Nana*, of c.1873 and 1877 respectively (RW 208 and 259), and the little portrait of Mallarmé (RW 249), painted in 1876). This suggests an earlier date than 1880–82 for the completion of the *Le jambon*, and a possibly still earlier date for the underlying composition.

Le jambon, like so many of Manet's pictures, was cut from a larger canvas. Judging from the underlying composition seen in the X-ray image, it was probably similar to still-lifes like *Le saumon (The salmon)*, a painting of 1869 (Shelburne Museum, Vermont, RW 140), which shows half a salmon on a dish, with a knife, a chianti flask and other objects on a linen tablecloth with heavy folds. The final background of *Le jambon* continues round the stretcher to the edges of the cut canvas, whereas the repainted surface of the tablecloth does not, and the picture may have been reworked more than once.

In *Le jambon*, Manet transformed a traditional type of still-life composition, by eliminating the anecdotal objects on the table and all the elements suggesting depth and recession. The ham is given a close-up, frontal presentation, accentuated by the flat background, the raised rear edge of the dish and the two thin lines which skate in anti-perspectival directions across the table and the picture surface. The composition is radically simplified and reduced to two main elements, balanced

18. I. *Le jambon*. Positive print from a composite X-radiograph of No. II (Fig. 19).

19. **II**. *Le jambon*. c.1875–78. 32.4 by 41.2 cm.
(The Burrell Collection, Glasgow.)

by the addition of Manet's swift, cursive signature over the painted-out object in the lower right corner.

This still-life painting is a good example of Manet's working methods, which remained essentially the same throughout his career. It shows the ways in which he worked towards simplification and clarity of design, so that in the end, this ham on a dish acquires the force and presence of a figure such as *Olympia* or the girl in the *Bar at the Folies-Bergère*.

Bathers and Picnics – The Early Nudes

Manet's first Salon paintings

The first work that Manet presented to the jury of the Paris Salon was the *Buveur d'absinthe*, rejected in 1859, when the artist was just twenty-seven. For the next Salon, in 1861, he successfully submitted the double portrait of his parents, and the *Espagnol jouant de la guitare* or *Chanteur espagnol*. The latter earned him a *mention honorable*, some critical acclaim and the admiration of a group of young painters, including Legros and Fantin-Latour. However, the 'realist' portrait and genre subject were only one aspect of the young artist's interests. The major subject of his early years was the female nude.

20. 1. Sketch for *La nymphe surprise* (see Fig.40). c.1858–60. Panel. 35.5 by 46 cm. (Nasjonalgalleriet, Oslo.) Col. ill. 3.

From 1863 the Salon became an annual event and Manet made his notorious entry on the scene with a huge painting he entitled first *Le bain*, and later *Le déjeuner sur l'herbe* (**19**, Fig.45). Rejected by the Salon jury, it was hung, in an excellent and eye-catching position,[1] in the famous Salon des Refusés, which opened, in rooms adjacent to the official Salon, on 15th May 1863. The picture provoked a storm of indignation, on the grounds of its alleged indecency as well as its manner of execution.

The *Déjeuner sur l'herbe* is dated 1863 and was therefore signed shortly before its submission to the jury. However, a Salon picture of this size was not painted overnight. There are many contemporary accounts and caricatures of artists working desperately during the months before the Salon opening to complete their pictures, and it was not unusual for the jury to extend the deadline for submissions. The origins of the *Déjeuner* stretch back over at least a year and more probably two, as can be shown by examining Manet's works on the theme of the seated and reclining nude. A fresh study of the *Déjeuner sur l'herbe* reveals an almost uninterrupted development from Manet's earliest recorded interest in these themes in the late 1850s.

Seated bather over reclining nude: Manet's first large painting project

Manet's first surviving design for a large-scale painting is known from an overall composition sketch, now in Oslo (**1**, Fig.20, Col.ill.3), generally known as *La nymphe surprise (*the *Surprised nymph)* or *Moïse sauvé des eaux (Moses saved from the waters)*. From the sketch, Manet painted a very large picture which he subsequently cut, saving only the part of the canvas with the seated bather or nymph, now in Buenos Aires (**2**, Fig.21). This fragment was exhibited by Manet in Russia, in 1861, with the title *Nymph and satyr*.[2] Although it has been assumed that the overall composition was the one referred to by Manet's life-long friend and biographer, Antonin Proust, as *Moses saved from the waters*,[3] this title is problematic, since a naked, bathing woman is hardly ever found in the presence of the Pharoah's daughter – conspicuously absent in the Oslo sketch – who is usually sumptuously attired and attended by her ladies-in-waiting (Figs.22 and 23).[4]

21. **2**. *Reclining nude*. Positive print from a composite X-radiograph of No.1 (Fig.20).

22. *Moïse sauvé*, by Edmé Jeaurat after Paolo Veronese. Engraving from the Recueil Crozat. (Bibliothèque Nationale, Cabinet des Estampes, Paris.)

23. *Moyse trouvé sur le Nil*, by Simon Vallée after Giovanni Francesco Romanelli. Engraving from the Recueil Crozat. (Bibliothèque Nationale, Cabinet des Estampes, Paris.)

In the hope of finding, beneath the much scraped and altered surface of the Oslo sketch, elements that would confirm Proust's identification of the subject, an X-radiograph was made (**2**, Fig. 21).[5] The underlying image it revealed came as a complete surprise: still clearly recognisable, in spite of severe scraping of the paint on the panel, is a reclining nude, with one knee drawn up. She emerges as Manet's earliest known encounter with the nude (apart from his direct copies after Titian), pre-dating, because underlying, the seated nude bather in the composition sketch on the surface (**1**, Fig. 20, Col. ill. 3) and pre-figuring the reclining, Titianesque nude later transformed by Manet into *Olympia* (**30**, Fig. 56).

The Oslo sketch panel therefore appears as the single starting point for two major sequences of works: the variations on the theme of the nude seated in a landscape that led to the *Déjeuner sur l'herbe* (**19**, Fig. 45), completed in 1863; and the theme of the Titianesque reclining nude that led, rather more directly, to *Olympia* (**30**, Fig. 56), dated the same year as the *Déjeuner* but shown at the Salon of 1865 and much more strikingly 'modern' in presentation and technique.

Both strands must have evolved simultaneously, and there were no doubt many related works of which all trace has been lost. We shall follow first one and then the other theme as they evolved over the years from around 1858 to 1863, starting with the *Nymphe – Déjeuner* sequence, since it shows a continuous progression and since, as will become clear, the *Déjeuner sur l'herbe* is in some ways more intimately related to the *Nymphe surprise* than is *Olympia* to her predecessor.

The missing Moses

Manet left the studio of Thomas Couture in 1856. At the end of the following year he was in Florence, and perhaps Rome, making copies after the works of the Italian masters, Titian (Fig. 54), Raphael, Andrea del Sarto, Luca della Robbia and many others.[6] In the winter of 1858, Manet registered at the Cabinet des Estampes in the then Bibliothèque impériale, where he almost certainly consulted the collections of reproductive prints after the Old Masters as well as the works of Rembrandt and the great original printmakers. Engravings and lithographs were still the most important type of reproductions available, photographs, although increasingly numerous in the second half of the nineteenth century, not yet being produced in large numbers.

24. **3**. *The finding of Moses*. c.1858–60. Pen and sepia ink with wash, over pencil, squared in red chalk, on joined sheets of smooth laid paper. 33.3 by 28 cm. (Museum Boymans-van Beuningen, Rotterdam.)

Antonin Proust, writing in 1897 (but, by his own account, from notes made over the years of his close friendship with Manet), stated that 'Manet began, in the rue Lavoisier [i.e. between 1856 and 1859], a large painting of *Moses saved from the waters* which he never completed'.[7] Although not iconographically identifiable with the Oslo sketch (1, Fig. 20, Col. ill. 3), the 'Moses saved' subject does appear in a remarkable early drawing by Manet. In pen and ink over pencil, on a patchwork of notebook sheets glued together by the artist and squared for transfer to canvas, it shows a kneeling woman who has just discovered the infant Moses in his basket (3, Fig. 24). It is, of course, possible that this drawing represents the whole composition originally intended by Manet, particularly since there are suggestions of a border line around the edges. But it seems more likely that this would have been just one motif in a large 'Moses' composition, which he may subsequently have altered until it became a *Nymphe surprise*.

Elements of the design of the Oslo sketch (1, Fig. 20, Col. ill. 3) are reminiscent of the Veronese and Romanelli 'Moses' compositions already mentioned (Figs. 22 and 23), and in the drawing there is also a suggestion of a river running down from a distant, mountainous horizon.[8]

Susannah, Bathsheba or just a surprised bather

Moses or no Moses, the principal element in the Oslo sketch composition (1, Fig. 20, Col. ill. 3) is the seated nude. This figure, for which many sources have been proposed, was developed in a series of drawings clearly made from the life (8–13, Figs. 33–38). The model was presumably Suzanne Leenhoff, the ample Dutch girl who gave piano lessons to the Manet brothers. In 1852 she gave birth to a son of uncertain fatherhood (but perhaps by Manet's own father).[9] Manet, who became the boy's godfather in 1855, was living with Suzanne by 1860, married her after the death of his father, in 1863, and treated the child, Léon (who was always presented as Suzanne's young brother), like a son.

The seated nude, clutching her towel to her and apparently hiding her nakedness from the indiscreet spectator, has been surprised while her maidservant combs out her hair after the bath. The pose recalls a classic 'Susannah' or 'Bathsheba' scene – the play on Suzanne's name has often been pointed out – and these subjects provide a generic source for some aspects of Manet's composition.

On one of Manet's early notebook pages is a drawing (4, Fig. 25) after a *David and Bathsheba* ceiling design by Giulio Romano for the Palazzo del Tè in Mantua.[10] The fresco composition is reversed in Manet's drawing, and was therefore almost certainly copied from the engraving of *Bathsheba at her bath* in a set of seventeenth-century engravings by Corneille le Jeune, that Manet could have seen in the Cabinet des Estampes (5, Fig. 26).[11] The second print in the set, showing *Bathsheba*

25. **4**. *Bathsheba*, by Manet after J. Corneille le Jeune and Giulio Romano (see Fig. 26). c.1858–60. Pencil on smooth laid paper, watermark *JOYNSON*. 17.8 by 13.2 cm. (Musée du Louvre, Cabinet des Dessins, Paris.)

26. **5**. *David spying upon Bathsheba*, by J. Corneille le Jeune after Giulio Romano. Engraving (composition reversed) after the fresco in the Palazzo del Tè, Mantua. 26 by 26 cm. (Bibliothèque Nationale, Cabinet des Estampes, Paris.)

27. **6**. *The toilet of Bathsheba*, by J. Corneille le Jeune after Giulio Romano. Engraving. 26 by 26 cm. (Bibliothèque Nationale, Cabinet des Estampes, Paris.)

25

26

27

28

28. *Head of a young woman (Suzanne Leenhoff).*
Red chalk on laid paper, watermark *NF.*
29.7 by 25.4 cm. (Bibliothèque Nationale,
Cabinet des Estampes, Paris.)

29. *La pêche.* c.1858–60. 76.8 by 123.2 cm.
(The Metropolitan Museum of Art,
New York.)

29

at her toilet (**6**, Fig. 27), also appears to be related to Manet's studies of the seated figure and her attendant, whose relationship he explored in the series of drawings already cited (**8–13**, Figs. 33–38), in both outdoor and indoor settings.

Since Suzanne Leenhoff was Manet's principal model at this period, it is interesting to note the close relationship of her physique to the Old Master models that Manet was following at the time. Besides Giulio Romano and Raphael,[12] Rubens is the artist to whom Manet specifically referred in one of his early paintings. In the costume picture entitled *La pêche*, he portrayed himself as Rubens and Suzanne as Hélène Fourment, in a composition borrowed from two of Rubens's landscapes (Fig. 29).[13]

The source most commonly cited for the surprised bather is Rubens's lost painting of *Susannah and the elders*, known from a reversed engraving by Vorstermann (**7**, Fig. 30), and also engraved for the article on Rubens in Charles Blanc's *Histoire des Peintres*.[14] Manet made several later portraits of Suzanne, but the earliest known is probably the handsome red chalk drawing in which she appears in profile, her lips parted, her hair partly braided and partly undone (Fig. 28), as in the *Susannah* after Rubens (**7**, Fig. 30).

Before exploring the development of the surprised bather composition and the sequence of drawings for which Suzanne Leenhoff was the model, it is worth

30. **7.** *Susannah and the elders*, by Lucas
Vorstermann after Rubens. Engraving.
39 by 27.8 cm. (British Museum, London.)
Reproduced in reverse.

31. *Seated nude.* c.1858–60. Positive print from
a composite X-radiograph of *Mlle Victorine
en costume d'espada* (Fig. 32).

32. *Mlle Victorine en costume d'espada.* Signed
and dated 1862. 165.1 by 127.6 cm. (The
Metropolitan Museum of Art, New York.)

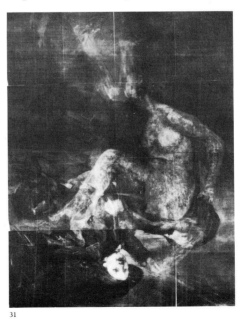

30

31

32

31

pointing out that Manet probably executed many related works that are lost or still 'hidden'. A life-size nude figure, posed much like his *Bathsheba* (**4**, Fig. 25) and possibly painted from Suzanne, appears, very surprisingly, in the inverted X-radiograph image of *Mlle V as an espada* (Figs. 31, 32),[15] an 1862 painting posed by his later model, Victorine Meurent, while drawings squared for transfer to canvas, as well as etchings without a known painted prototype (see **10** and **14**, Figs. 35, 39) suggest how fragmentary our knowledge of Manet's original *œuvre* may be.[16] There are several records of his destruction of paintings which no longer satisfied him; we know that he often cut and repainted his canvases; and it is evident from studying the few pages that have survived from a large number of sketchbooks that we have only a fraction of his output as a draughtsman.[17] Proust and other friends emphasised over and over again how Manet constantly consigned in his sketchbooks everything he observed around him. Apart from such basic notations, there must have been many studies for all the early paintings (not a single one is known for the *Déjeuner sur l'herbe*), and composition or figure sketches for the later ones.

Five nude bathers sitting in a row

The striking sequence of five drawings of a nude bather is assembled here for the first time, together with a unique engraved mica 'tracing' of one of them and the etching made from another (**8–14**, Figs. 33–39). Apart from showing the range of Manet's graphic techniques, the sequence also charts an essential development in his art. The whole composition of the Oslo sketch (**1**, Fig. 20, Col. ill. 3), its principal sources (**5–7**, Figs. 26–30) and Manet's related works, including the two wash drawings (**8** and **9**, Figs. 33, 34) that were probably the earliest in the sequence of

33. **8**. *Seated bather, facing right (I)*. c.1858–60. Pen and sepia ink with wash over red chalk, on thin wove paper (laid down). 26.7 by 19.9 cm. (Museum Boymans-van Beuningen, Rotterdam.)

34. **9**. *Seated bather, facing right (II)*. c.1858–60. Pen and sepia ink with wash over red chalk, with black chalk corrections, on thin wove paper. 26.5 by 20.4 cm. (Private collection, London.)

35. **10**. *Seated bather, with both arms raised*. c.1858–60. Red chalk with pencil corrections, squared in pencil, on laid paper, watermark *NF*. 30.9 by 25.5 cm. (Bibliothèque Nationale, Cabinet des Estampes, Paris.)

36. **11**. *Seated bather, with left arm raised*. c.1858–60. Red chalk on laid paper, watermark *NF*. 26.6 by 23 cm. (The Art Institute of Chicago.) Col. ill. 1.

33

34

35

36

37

37. **12.** *Seated bather, with left arm raised.*
c.1858–60. Incised mica sheet with black
chalk touches on the face. 23.7 by 15.9 cm.
(Musée du Louvre, Cabinet des Dessins,
Paris.)

five, are full of intense energy expressed in movement, or dramatically arrested
movement. After these, there is a progressive development, perhaps through a
lost intermediate composition (see **10**, Fig. 35), towards a much stabler, quieter
type of design. Echoes of Romanelli, Giulio Romano and Rubens give way to the
tranquillity of Titian and the Venetian masters and to the kind of painting to
which Proust referred when he recorded Manet's preference for *'les choses claires
et les sujets tranquilles'*.

The two wash drawings (**8** and **9**, Figs. 33, 34) have an almost Rembrandtesque
vigour and spontaneity, and the second version (**9**, Fig. 34) has a sensitivity and an
element of mystery that belies the economy of means. The model is seen as if 'out
of doors', with a suggestion of strong sunlight and shadow, and although the pose
is reversed in the Oslo oil sketch (**1**, Fig. 20), there is the same feeling of surprise, of
a figure caught unawares. This is reinforced in the second drawing by the correction
in black chalk which brings the woman's right arm up and across her belly.[18]

In all the drawings in this sequence, as well as the etching (**14**, Fig. 39), the nude
figure is virtually the same size, and corresponds with the size of the bather in the
Oslo sketch (**1**, Fig. 20, Col. ill. 3). A drawing in red chalk, with strong lead pencil
corrections to the head and arms, is squared for transfer (**10**, Fig. 35). It is impossible
to tell whether it was intended for the outdoor *Nymphe surprise* composition or the
interior *Toilette* scene recorded in Manet's etching (**14**, Fig. 39). The same appears
true of the superb red chalk drawing in Chicago, in which the attendant maidservant also appears, in alternative positions marked by numerous pentimenti,
either combing her mistress's hair or preparing to clothe her (**11**, Fig. 36, Col. ill. 1).
Here, however, there is a suggestion, at lower right, of the basin that also appears
in *La toilette* (**13** and **14**, Figs. 38, 39), so the setting is probably an interior one. On

a gelatine or 'mica' sheet (**12**, Fig. 37), Manet engraved the traced outline of the nude from the Chicago sheet (retouching it with black chalk on the face), presumably in order to transfer it as the basis for a further study. The 'final' design – drawn and etched by Manet (**13** and **14**, Figs. 38, 39) – most probably existed at one time as a painting. Proust recorded a picture with the title *La toilette* among the series of *études* executed between 1858 and 1860, together with *The Salamanca students*, *Moses saved from the waters* and *The promenade*.[19]

If the Chicago drawing is a study for the *Toilette* composition, the drawing, also in red chalk, in the Courtauld Collection (**13**, Fig. 38) was certainly made in preparation for the etching. Its summary outlines are slashed right through the sheet where Manet traced over them with a stylus to transfer his design to the copperplate for etching. This method, which transferred the image directly to the plate, resulted in a reversed image when the plate was printed (**14**, Fig. 39). The etching was published in a set of Manet's prints in 1862, with the title *La toilette*. The sparseness of the preparatory drawing, in contrast to the richly elaborated interior scene of the etching, in itself suggests that Manet must have had a more complete image to work from. That this image was a painting is supported by Proust's statement, by the fact that almost all Manet's early prints were copies of his paintings (including works he later destroyed, such as the painting of *Les gitanos*), and even by the curious framing line drawn through the bather's knees. This suggests an attempt to find a new format for the picture, if he was dissatisfied and contemplating altering it. Whether the putative picture was destroyed or painted over, like the nude study (Figs. 31, 32), only systematic X-radiographic examination of Manet's canvases will show.

38. **13**. *La toilette*. c.1860–61. Red chalk on laid paper, watermark *NF*, incised for transfer. 29.1 by 21 cm. (Courtauld Institute Galleries, London.)

39. **14**. *La toilette*. c.1860–61. Etching. 28.7 by 22.5 cm. (British Museum, London.)

40. **15**. *La nymphe surprise*. Signed and dated 1861. Photograph by Godet, showing the satyr's head among the trees. 1872. 32 by 26 cm. (Bibliothèque Nationale, Cabinet des Estampes, Paris.)

41. **16**. *La nymphe surprise*. Positive print from a composite X-radiograph of No.15 (Fig.40), showing the over-painted, cut figure on the left (see No.1, Fig.20), and the maid behind the seated nude. (Museo Nacional de Bellas Artes, Buenos Aires.)

La Nymphe surprise

From small sketch to large-scale canvas

X-radiographs of the large Buenos Aires painting (**15** and **16**, Figs.40, 41), have confirmed that it is indeed a fragment of a huge canvas based on the Oslo sketch (**1**, Fig.20, Col. ill.3). Part of the figure who is seen running off into the distance in the sketch appears at the left edge of the large, cut canvas, and the attendant maidservant is visible in the X-ray image, moved slightly to the right and busy with the bather's hair. The original composition, as far as one can judge from the present state of the sketch, was a free variation on high renaissance, and particularly Venetian, themes. The broad landscape setting with a distant vista rising to a mountain range, under a blue and white summer sky, is a classic Arcadian setting such as Manet studied in Titian's *Venus del Pardo* in the Louvre, then known as *Jupiter and Antiope* (**17**, Fig.42). Manet made a small copy of the painting (Fig.43) and could have studied its motifs more closely (it was in very poor condition and heavily repainted) in the large and detailed engraved reproduction in the Crozat *recueil* (**20**, Fig.46).

42

42. **17**. *Venus del Pardo* (formerly called *Jupiter and Antiope*), by Titian. 196 by 385 cm. (Musée du Louvre, Paris. INV 752.) Photograph by Alinari c.1890–1900. (Musée du Louvre, Documentation du Département des Peintures.)

43. *Venus del Pardo* (formerly called *Jupiter and Antiope*), by Manet after Titian. c.1857–60. 47 by 85 cm. (Formerly Rouart Collection, Paris.)

Indeed, this reversed engraving after Titian is remarkably similar, in its disposition of the open landscape on the left and copse of trees on the right, not only to the Oslo sketch composition (**1**, Fig. 20) but also to the landscape of *La pêche* (Fig. 29),[20] where the suburban landscape stands in for Arcady and Suzanne's son Léon, fishing, takes the place of the hunt, and where even the naked figures under the distant trees[21] find a prototype in the centre of Titian's composition.

The nymph cut out of her canvas and satyrised

Manet's apparent difficulty in adjusting his figures within this landscape setting presumably led him to abandon this huge canvas. He cut out the figure of the bather – approximately two-fifths of the width of the original picture (as estimated in proportion to the Oslo sketch) – and transformed her setting. The remains of the figure on the left were painted out and replaced by the suggestion of a pool or river; the bather's attendant was suppressed and Manet created a more suitable foil for the solid forms of the nude by replacing the slender trees with much more sturdy trunks and a mass of green foliage that corresponds with the original position of the maidservant in the Oslo sketch (**1**, Fig. 20, Col. ill. 3).

As to the satyr, he was lightly brushed in to complete the picture before it was sent to the exhibition in St Petersburg, and his head is just visible in the photographs taken by Godet in 1872 (**15**, Fig. 40),[22] and by Lochard in 1883,[23] thus proving that the satyr was eliminated after Manet's death.

With the satyr's head among the branches, the nude was indisputably a *nymphe surprise*. But until that moment, her status was ambiguous and she could have been simply a girl shivering a little after her dip in the river. Her gaze, turned towards the spectator, indicates little more than the calm interest in the viewer-voyeur beyond the picture plane shown by Tintoretto's *Susannah* in the Louvre, as she continues with her toilet.[24] This same ambiguity runs through the development of the painting Manet was first to exhibit as *Le bain*, where the final form of the composition was evidently very much at variance with the anodyne title of the work.

Le Déjeuner sur l'herbe

Arcadian origins

As implied at the beginning of this section, Manet's great *Déjeuner sur l'herbe* (**19**, Fig. 45) cannot have been painted in the space of a few months. X-radiographs made specially on the occasion of this study of the artist's working methods have produced startlingly unexpected – and beautiful – results (**18**, Fig. 44).[25] Beneath the enclosed forest glade lies an enchanting, airy, Arcadian landscape, almost identical with the one glimpsed in the sketch for the *Nymphe surprise* (**1**, Fig. 20, Col. ill. 3), and also very similar to that in *La pêche* (Fig. 29).

The slim saplings are there behind the figures, and to the left is the distant vista with a mountain range, beneath a summer sky enlivened by white clouds. The grass is full of flowers, with water plants similar to those at the bather's feet in the large *Nymphe surprise* painting (**15**, Fig. 40), down in the lower left corner; and there even appears to be a dog – a somewhat scraped and now headless animal – just behind the nude figure's back. In the composition as it appears in the X-ray image, Manet seems to have welded into the landscape taken from the engraving after Titian's *Jupiter and Antiope* (**20**, Fig. 46), his figure group based on Marcantonio's engraving after Raphael (**21**, Fig. 47), modified with reference to yet another print from the Crozat *recueil*, after Giorgione's *Pastorale*, now known as the Titian-Giorgione *Concert champêtre* (**22**, Fig. 48).[26]

Old Master sources – prints v. paintings

It may seem fanciful to suggest that these paintings owed so much to the engravings in the Crozat *recueil*, but the relevance of the reversed images in the engravings appears to support the view that they may have been almost as important to Manet as his study of the darkened paintings themselves in the Louvre.[27] Even the 'picnic' elements in the great Titian composition – the fruit and wine jar – have a crispness and legibility in the engraving which would have been far more suggestive to Manet, in their details, than the corresponding area in the dark and repainted canvas (**17** and **20**, Figs. 42, 46). And if the Marcantonio engraving (**21**, Fig. 47) was of such basic importance for the posing of his live models, the other prints may well have been equally important as sources for the setting and the general compositional scheme.

Of these Old Master sources, only the Titian-Giorgione *Concert champêtre* moves away from the antique world of gods and nymphs and satyrs. There, the two naked women are in the company of youths in contemporary 'period' dress, and even the strong elements of Arcadian allegory cannot counteract the equally strong sense of contemporaneity and immediacy that the image presents. In Manet's painting of *Le bain*, or *Le déjeuner sur l'herbe*, there is a decisive move away from the classical world of make-believe and into a vivid and – to the public of his day – shockingly modern context.

From a nude nymph to a naked young woman

In the early state of the *Déjeuner sur l'herbe* as seen in the X-ray image (**18**, Fig. 44), Manet's model poses as the Raphael-Marcantonio nymph (see **21**, Fig. 47), seated on a piece of drapery, with the Titian-derived picnic beside her. As yet she is only a nymph, and has no discarded clothes. Or at the most, she belongs to the ambiguous, Arcadian world between reality and the ideal, seen in the Titian-Giorgione design (**22**, Fig. 48). In the X-ray image of Manet's painting, reeds and rushes grow where, in the final state (**19**, Fig. 45), Victorine Meurent's spotted muslin dress and be-

ribboned straw hat will lie. Only during the last stages of the picture's execution, with the addition of the discarded clothes, did she become a thoroughly and explicitly modern figure.

We shall probably never know exactly when Manet began his painting of the *Déjeuner sur l'herbe*, or when he transformed his composition; whether it was begun even before he cut and transformed the canvas of the *Nymphe surprise* (**15**, Fig. 40) – the alterations he makes are virtually the same in both, down to the thick mass of greenery added behind the nude in the *Déjeuner*; and whether the final alterations to the landscape and the addition of the clothes on the grass were made early on or only shortly before he submitted the picture to the Salon jury. This raises an important question about the model. Was Victorine, whom Manet met in 1862, the only model who posed for the nude in the *Déjeuner sur l'herbe*, or was she preceded by an earlier model whom Manet subsequently transformed? The same question will be discussed in relation to the painting of *Olympia* (**30**, Fig. 56), but it can be noted here that the X-ray image of the nude in the *Déjeuner* shows that Manet reworked the figure considerably, and that within the pose established by the Marcantonio engraving there are many slight shifts in the position and outline of the nude.

44. **18**. *Le déjeuner sur l'herbe*. Positive print from a composite X-radiograph of No. **19** (Fig. 45), showing the wide, open landscape to the left, the slender trees, and the plants in place of Victorine's clothes.

45. **19**. *Le déjeuner sur l'herbe*. Signed and
dated 1863. 208 by 264 cm., originally
214 by 270 cm. (Musée d'Orsay – Galeries
du Jeu de Paume, Paris.)

The later 'Déjeuners'

Whatever the sequence of its development may have been, the evidence of the
X-ray image of Manet's *Déjeuner* serves to confirm the view that his water-colour
(**23**, Fig. 49) was made from the painting in its final form, and was not a study for
the composition. It also places the Courtauld picture (**24**, Fig. 50) at least after the
first version of the composition, and probably after the final state. One of Manet's
major problems with the *Déjeuner* was evidently his difficulty in integrating the
very solid, sculptural figure group into the original open and airy setting. In the
finished state of his Salon painting, the alterations to the setting help to provide a
stronger and more stable context for the figures, just as in the *Nymphe surprise*.
The Courtauld picture appears to take this process a stage further and creates, in a
curiously harsh and hasty style to which it is very difficult to assign a date, a more
coherent, close-knit relationship between the foreground figures, while reducing
the scale and improving the perspective view of the bather in the background.

In this necessarily hypothetical reconstruction of the possible chain of events,
Manet's '*Moïse sauvé – Nymphe surprise*' composition nevertheless appears as the
direct predecessor, indissolubly linked to the development of the *Déjeuner sur
l'herbe*. We must now explore the second strand that leads from the small Oslo
sketch panel, and follow the earlier incarnations of *Olympia*.

Jupiter amoureux d'Antiope se transforme en Satire

46

47

Pastorale

48

46. **20**. *Jupiter amoureux d'Antiope se transforme
en Satire*, by Bernard Baron after Titian's
Venus del Pardo (No.**17**, Fig.42). Engraving
(reversed composition) from the Recueil
Crozat. 38.7 by 66.3 cm. (British Museum,
London.)

47. **21**. *The judgment of Paris*, by Marcantonio
Raimondi after Raphael. Engraving. 29.5 by
44.3 cm. (British Museum, London.)

48. **22**. *Pastorale*, by Nicolas Dupuy after
Giorgione (now known as *Le concert
champêtre*, attributed to Titian). Engraving
(reversed composition, see No.**17**, Fig.42)
from the Recueil Crozat. 33 by 38.5 cm.
(British Museum, London.)

49. **23**. *Le déjeuner sur l'herbe*. c.1863–65. Pen and ink and watercolour over pencil, on laid paper, watermark *J WHATMAN*. 40.8 by 48 cm. (The Ashmolean Museum, Oxford.)

50. **24**. *Le déjeuner sur l'herbe*. c.1864–68? 89.5 by 116 cm. (Courtauld Institute Galleries, London.)

51. **25**. *Reclining nude*. c.1857–59. Red chalk on laid paper. 24.7 by 45.7 cm. (Musée du Louvre, Cabinet des Dessins, Paris.) Col. ill. 2.

Olympia

The hidden nude

The shadowy reclining nude that emerges in the X-radiographs of the Oslo sketch (**1** and **2**, Figs. 20, 21) seems to have been painted with the help of a drawing (**25**, Fig. 51, Col. ill. 2) generally considered to be a study for *Olympia* (**30**, Fig. 56). The large red chalk nude corresponds almost exactly with what can be seen of the figure on the painted panel, both in outline and in actual size.

In the study, no doubt drawn from life, the model reclines against a large pillow; her right forearm is raised so that her hand rests on the collarbone; her left arm is extended, with the hand resting on her drawn-up right knee (the outline of the knee is continuous, and the hand may or may not have been in that position originally). The head is left absolutely featureless, but the hair is indicated with a centre parting and appears to be bound, rather than loose.

This drawing is in turn very closely related to a smaller study (**26**, Fig. 52), squared for transfer to a canvas, in which the model lies in almost exactly the same pose, but her left arm is not visible. In this version, she has distinct, though very generalised features, and her hair is clearly braided and pinned around her head. There is a suggestion of drapery lying over and around her thighs. In neither drawing is there any indication of a setting, beyond the inclusion of a pillow.

See Fig. 21.

52. **26**. *Reclining nude*. c.1857–59. Red chalk, squared, on laid paper, watermark *NF*. 22.5 by 30 cm. (Bibliothèque Nationale, Cabinet des Estampes, Paris.)

Who was the model?

The girl in these two drawings has always been identified as Victorine Meurent, a young professional model whom Manet began to use from 1862, and who undoubtedly appears in the *Déjeuner sur l'herbe* and *Olympia*, besides many other paintings of the early 1860s. Given the generalised nature of the figures, it will probably be impossible to determine whether Victorine in fact posed for one or both of these apparently early drawings. If they were indeed made for the first painting on the Oslo panel (**2**, Fig.21), as the similar dimensions of the larger drawing suggest, they cannot be later than 1858– 59, by which date Manet must have painted the *Moïse sauvé – Nymphe surprise* composition sketch that covered over the nude. Certainly neither drawing suggests the ample forms of Suzanne Leenhoff, but we know from an early notebook that Manet was on the look-out for good models (noting down their names and addresses and physical type),[28] and it would be surprising if he had used no model other than Suzanne in the preceding years.

Although one cannot entirely agree with Tabarant that these drawings are simply academic nudes and 'have nothing to do with *Olympia*',[29] their style certainly suggests a date before 1860 and the pose of the figure in both the drawings and the 'hidden' painting is extremely significant if they are seen as an early idea for a large reclining nude.

An antique or modern heroine?
From Danaë and Venus to Olympia

Reclining nudes in high renaissance Venetian art fall into two principal groups: Venus and Danaë. The goddess Venus usually lies peacefully, stretched out on a couch or on the ground, asleep or quietly dreamy, attended by Cupid, handmaidens or an importunate satyr (**17** and **20**, Figs.42, 46, 54).[30] Danaë's story focuses on her one moment of glory, when Jupiter visited her in the form of a shower of golden rain; she is shown lying on a couch, with her knees drawn up and thighs parted to receive the god, gazing up expectantly (**27**, Figs.52a, 53).[31]

Manet's early figure is virtually an amalgam of the two poses, though the hand raised to the throat appears to be a motif of his own invention.[32] But already his

52a. *Danaë*, by Gauchard from a drawing by Cabasson after Titian (Museo di Capodimonte, Naples). Wood-engraving, 9.6 by 13.7 cm. In Charles Blanc, *Histoire des peintres*, 'Titian', p.11. (Bibliothèque Nationale, Cabinet des Estampes, Paris.)

53. **27**. *Danaë*, by Louis Desplaces after Titian. Engraving (composition reversed) from the Recueil Crozat. 25.5 by 33 cm. (British Museum, London.) Reproduced in the same sense as the painting.

figure shows the cool detachment that is so characteristic of *Olympia* (**30**, Fig. 56): there is neither the dreamy sensuality of Titian's Venus nor the more ardent intensity of Danaë. Manet's model is awake and holds her head high, though her gaze is apparently not yet directed towards the spectator, as was, for example, Ingres's *Grande odalisque*'s (Louvre, Paris) and many other reclining nudes of the early and mid-nineteenth century.

Manet copied Titian's *Jupiter and Antiope* or *Venus del Pardo* in the Louvre (**17**, Figs. 42, 43); and presumably in Florence in the winter of 1857, he made a similar small copy (**28**, Fig. 54) of Titian's *Venus of Urbino* in the Uffizi.[33] If one supposes that the reclining nude drawings (**25** and **26**, Figs. 51, 52, Col. ill. 2) and the underlying painting on the Oslo panel (**2**, Fig. 21) were made on his return to Paris, before he set to work on the *Moses – Nymph* composition, there is no known surviving work to show how the theme developed – in his mind, on paper or on canvas – until *Olympia* (**30**, Fig. 56) sprang into view, signed and dated in 1863.[34]

54. **28**. *Venus of Urbino*, by Manet after Titian. 1857? Panel. 24 by 37 cm. (Private collection.)

Olympia's transformation – the X-ray image

The only element to hand, in the attempt to establish the development that led from the reclining nude of *c.*1858 to *Olympia* in 1863, is the X-radiograph of the Salon painting (**29** and **30**; Figs. 55, 56). The X-ray image is rather hard to read, but it clearly reveals several interesting changes. First and perhaps most important, the head of Olympia show signs of strong scraping and reworking, and it is not inconceivable that Victorine came to replace an earlier model, and that the large canvas could therefore have originated before Manet met Victorine in 1862.

Second, there appear to have been considerable changes in the setting. The diagonal, forward movement of the attendant negress was originally echoed by a draped curtain, beyond which a light area suggests a more distant perspective. The negress's torso was not obscured by the extravagant paper wrapping of the bouquet (through which the pink of her dress still shows) and the wrapped bouquet was much smaller. Moreover, the black girl's forms were more ample and her dress extended to the left, disappearing behind the centre of Olympia's thigh (rather than at her knee, as at present).[35]

In the final version of Manet's painting, the negress presents a far more sumptuous and eye-catching 'offering' to her mistress, and her chocolate-brown hand is an addition which brilliantly highlights the huge and much-derided paper wrapping added around the bouquet of flowers. The bouquet itself remained untouched, the primed but unpainted canvas serving as the background to the flowers (and therefore reading 'black' in the X-radiograph).

Although the lighter area behind the negress is virtually illegible in the X-radiograph and appears to have been strongly scraped – one assumes it showed a view analogous to that in the *Venus of Urbino* (**28**, Fig. 54) – it serves to show up the alterations in the foreground, and particularly at the foot of the bed. This was differently finished and draped (indeed, the drapery of the sheets appears to have been modified throughout, to smooth and simplify their almost baroque folds). There are signs of much scraping and alteration around the feet and there were very probably no slippers originally, nor is it certain that the embroidered shawl was present on the bed, at least in its final form. The relaxed right hand, with the index finger pointing down, does not appear to be fingering anything; there are indications (clearer on the picture than in the X-radiograph) suggesting that the outline of the buttock may have been visible; and a fold of drapery appears originally to have passed between the legs, halfway below the knee.

Not only is there no trace of the famous black cat (the dark pigment would not show up in an X-ray) but there is no indication of the sort of 'platform' on which it stands, whereas two rounded shapes suggest that there could have been the kind of little dog that lies sleeping at the feet of Titian's *Venus of Urbino* (see Fig. 54). The bracelet (which adorns Titian's Venus and Danaë figures), shows alterations in its outline and in the X-ray image does not yet appear to have the pendant stone – the bracelet worn by Victorine as Olympia belonged to Manet's family and contained a lock of the artist's baby hair[36] – and it is not clear whether there was originally the famous black velvet ribbon around Venus-Victorine's throat.

Olympia's modernity

In other words, the elements that make *Olympia* an essentially modern image, the attributes and trappings that so shockingly emphasised her status as a contemporary prostitute in the eyes of the Salon public, seem to be absent in the underlying version of the picture which is shown, in the X-radiograph image, to be far closer to its Titianesque models. This in itself suggests that the painting may have been started at an earlier date than has been suspected, when Manet stayed closer to Old Master prototypes. Comparison of the earlier and later states of *Olympia* shows Manet moving away from a more traditional representation in which the two-dimensional emphasis of the horizontal nude is lessened by the three-dimensional elements of the bed, the ample shape of the negress and the suggestion of a perspective view behind her. In the final state – which may even have been arrived at after he had signed and dated the painting in 1863[37] – Manet achieved a supremely accomplished fusion of elements of Titian's *Venus of Urbino* with those of his own invention: the closed-off, almost stifling setting, divided into flat planes (thus solving his constant problems with spatial recession, already seen in the *Déjeuner sur l'herbe*); the extended, tellingly crisp outlines of the bouquet in the negress's arms; the precisely defined psychological and pictorial relationships between the figures; and, of course, the cat. With all these modifications, Manet achieved an

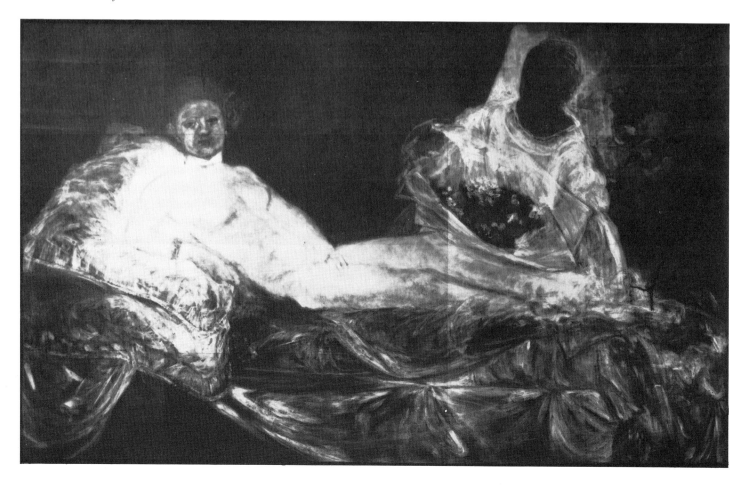

even more spectacular leap into 'modernity' than the one marked, in an analogous way, by the addition of the cast-off clothes to the *Déjeuner sur l'herbe* (**19**, Fig. 45), which completed the transformation of his nude, still identifiable as a 'modern nymph', into a shameless and unmistakably modern young woman. As for *Olympia*, her very name wittily combines an antique resonance with echoes of the contemporary *demi-monde*.

55. **29**. *Olympia*. Positive print from a partial composite X-radiograph of No. 30 (Fig. 56).

From the Oslo panel derive two major subjects that Manet developed simultaneously. He made two versions of the open-air scene – with the *Nymphe surprise* composition leading to the final statement of the *Déjeuner* – and may have transformed the original Danaë-Venus nude directly on the canvas until she became Olympia.[38] At all events, the development of this reclining nude subject, as far as it can be deduced from the evidence available, throws light on Manet's decisive move towards the construction of a richly two-dimensional (rather than three-dimensional) type of painting, allied to an emphatically 'modern' subject.

Manet's post-Olympian progress

In 1862, Manet had already completed *Musique aux Tuileries* (National Gallery, London); he was about to paint the very large, lost racecourse scene, *Aspect d'une course au bois de Boulogne*[39] and the brilliant piece of reportage that was perhaps also a political gesture on his part, the *Battle of the 'Kearsarge' and the 'Alabama'*.[40] Both of these date from 1864. The following year, after the fiasco of the exhibition of *Olympia* at the Salon of 1865, he went to Spain and was spellbound by the paintings of Velázquez. In 1866 his Salon entries (*Le fifre* and *L'acteur tragique*, both deeply influenced by Velázquez) were refused,[41] and in protest Manet opened his studio to the public during the period of the Salon.

The following year, 1867, fearing rejection from the Salon held in conjunction

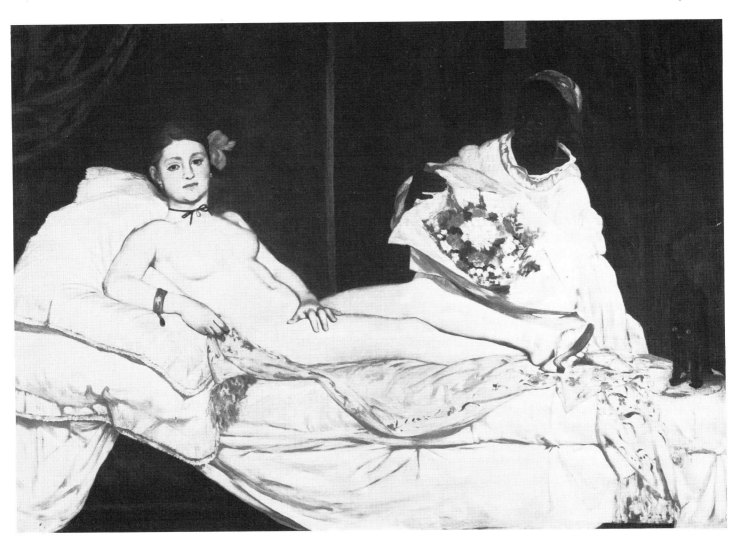

56. **30**. *Olympia*. Signed and dated 1863.
130.5 by 190 cm. (Musée d'Orsay – Galeries
du Jeu de Paume, Paris.)

with the Exposition universelle, he, like Courbet, held his own one-man exhibition in a specially-built pavilion near the grounds of the Exposition. He issued a brief catalogue, listing the fifty-three paintings displayed and stating his point of view in an elegantly phrased preface (quoted above, p.3). He also published a brochure, with a long essay by Zola and an etching after *Olympia* made specially for the occasion.

Then, in June, came the event which was to launch him on a new series of works as important and as complex in their development as the early nude compositions: the execution of the Emperor Maximilian in Mexico, which inspired Manet's three great history paintings on this theme.

The Execution of Maximilian

On 19th June 1867, at Querétaro (to the north-west of Mexico City), the Austrian Archduke Maximilian, Emperor of Mexico, with two Mexican generals who had remained faithful to him, was shot by the nationalist guerrilla troops of Benito Juárez.

Maximilian had accepted the throne of Mexico in April 1864, entering into a pact with Napoleon III who already had an army of occupation in Mexico and hoped to subdue the country and extend his empire overseas with the help of a 'legitimate' puppet Emperor.[42] In February 1867, following the victory of the Union forces in the Civil War in the United States and Bismarck's increasing threat to France in Europe, Napoleon III decided to betray the express terms of his agreement with Maximilian and withdraw all French troops from Mexico.

Maximilian was left with his own small army, a mixed group of trustworthy and traitorous generals, and his quixotic blend of romantic illusion and great personal courage. He chose to fight the Republican forces of Juárez, retreating from Mexico City to Querétaro where he was caught in a trap, besieged and eventually betrayed and captured on 16th May 1867. The Emperor was 'tried', with Miguel Miramón, his chief of infantry and a former rival President to Juárez, and Tomás Mejía, a loyal Indian general, and on 19th June all three were executed by firing squad (see Figs. 63–66).

The news reached Europe on 30th June and the official announcement was conveyed to Napoleon III on the inappropriate occasion of the prize-giving ceremony at the Exposition universelle. The great world's fair, staged on the banks of the Seine at the Pont de l'Alma, was depicted by Manet[43] who, like Courbet, had set up a pavilion just outside the grounds of the official Exposition and was showing a magnificent retrospective exhibition of his own work to a largely uninterested public. Manet was a convinced Republican and vigorous critic of the policies and character of Napoleon III, and like all French liberals he must have followed the reports of the Mexican affair and been forming his own opinion concerning the probable outcome. The dramatic *dénouement* filled the press with both factual and fictional reports and images, and one wonders whether Manet, in taking a current sensation as a subject for a major painting, did not originally intend to present it in the ready-made context of his own exhibition pavilion,[44] before deciding to turn it into a major Salon painting.

Manet's 'Maximilian' series re-examined

Between June 1867 and January 1869, Manet made three separate attempts to bring off a great contemporary history painting, only to come up against the authorities' determination to prevent the exhibition of the final version of the picture and the publication of his lithograph of the same subject.

The three large paintings (31, 32 and 37, Figs. 57, 60/61 and 71, Col. ill. 11), an oil sketch (35, Fig. 69, Col. ill. 10) and the lithograph (34, Fig. 68) have been analysed many times in an attempt to unravel their sequence, to understand their relationship to newspaper accounts and images of the event and the personalities involved, and to identify Manet's sources for the construction of his composition, with their implications for an understanding of his attitudes to the scene he was depicting.[45]

In 1983, on the occasion of the Manet exhibition at the National Gallery, London, permission was sought to X-ray the oil sketch from Copenhagen, which showed evident signs of having been extensively reworked (**33** and **35**, Figs.67 and 69, Col. ill.10).[46] At the same time, studies independently undertaken at the museum in Copenhagen resulted in publication of the X-radiograph evidence together with a detailed physical description of the canvas and analysis of its composition in relation to the other works.[47] The new evidence afforded by the sketch led to a fresh examination of the final version of the composition in Mannheim and ultimately to its transportation to the Doerner Institute in Munich for full examination and restoration (**36** and **37**, Figs.70, 71, Col. ill.11). The existing X-radiographs of parts of the London version were re-examined, and the first version, in the Boston Museum of Fine Arts, has also recently been X-radiographed (**31** and **31a**, Figs.57, 58).[48] It is thus now possible to lay out all the new evidence, so that a fresh assessment of the entire sequence of Manet's works on the theme may be attempted.

The First Version: Boston

In spite of its large size, the Boston version of the *Execution of Maximilian* (**31**, Fig.57) is very much an *ébauche*, or first draft, full of unresolved corrections and difficult to read in many areas. It is generally agreed that Manet probably painted it shortly after the news of the execution reached Europe, but before full reports came through with precise details of the event, eye-witness accounts were published and authentic documents described in the press.

The newspaper reports

The information for Manet's first depiction of the scene may have come from the account in *Le Figaro* of 8th July 1867, in which the following elements were reported: the prisoners left for the place of execution at 7a.m.; the procession climbed the hill leading to the cemetery, with impressive views over the surrounding plain; the road was barred to prevent the crowd following the procession up the hill; three benches with wooden crosses were placed against the great wall surrounding the cemetery; three firing squads, each consisting of five men with two officers to give the *coup de grâce*, advanced to within three paces of the condemned men; Maximilian embraced his companions, took leave of the bishop and abbot who had accompanied them, and spoke words which brought tears to many eyes; he then stepped forward and addressed the commanding officer; on a sword signal, the muskets fired into his chest and he was heard to speak in German as smoke enveloped the spectators; Miramón, who had been slumped on a bench, collapsed instantly; Mejía remained standing, thrashing the air with his arms until a bullet in his ear finished him off.[49]

Between 8th July and 10th October 1867, many newspaper reports gave varying accounts of the scene and Manet certainly followed these reports with interest and modified his composition, at least in some details. However, the most striking thing about Manet's whole sequence of works devoted to the execution of Maximilian is that he never basically altered the design of the Boston composition. In spite of an endless catalogue of 'sources', no one has yet found a single, specific model for the composition. It is in many ways very far, at least in its later versions, from the most universally acknowledged source, Goya's painting of the *Executions of the Third of May 1808* (see Fig.59), which must have been seen by Manet in Madrid in 1865. It was then, with its pendant *The second of May*, in the Royal Museum (now the

57

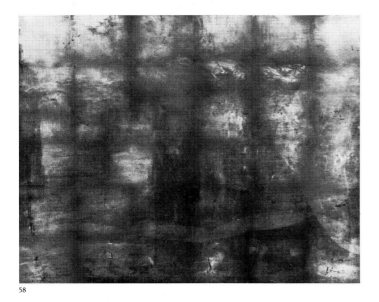

58

59

50

Prado), and in 1867 Charles Yriarte described Goya's execution scene as one of his most celebrated works. He published an engraved reproduction of it (Fig. 59) in his major study of Goya's life and work, which appeared in Paris in April 1867, two months before the events in Mexico. Manet is also known to have owned a set of Goya's etchings of the *Disasters of War*, and although he expressed no great admiration for Goya's paintings,[50] he may have been more impressed by his prints and by the striking reproduction of the *Third of May*, just published in Paris. In the final analysis, Manet's design was no doubt based as much on general patterns of representations of an execution, and his own deeply felt response to the accounts of the drama, as on any specific source.

Manet's first design

The summary of the principal events of the execution, as narrated in the *Figaro* article, suggests how far Manet chose to follow or to disregard specific, reported details of the event at this early stage. Already, in the Boston version (**31**, Fig. 57), the composition is conceived as a unified, symbolic act: the execution of the Emperor and his generals by only one firing squad, under its officer, accompanied by the non-commissioned officer who was to give the *coup de grâce*. In an unspecific setting, with just a suggestion of rising ground behind the figures, a compact group of soldiers, five or perhaps more in number, is firing at very close range at the victims. Mejía, on the left, can already be identified from the gesture of his arm and hand, tautened and 'thrashing' while his head falls forward on his chest. The Emperor, a tall, bearded figure wearing a sombrero, appears to have taken one step forward, as indicated in the report; he stands erect, a flat-brimmed sombrero on his head (see Fig. 65), his face and fair beard rising above a puff of white smoke. Of the third figure, reported as being seated, there are no more than the sketchiest indications beside the Emperor.

The executed are set back from the executioners. In the right foreground, counteracting this perspective effect and tying the scene to the picture plane, are two figures: the frontally-posed N.C.O. charging his rifle to end the victims' agony if necessary, and the officer, almost cut off by the right edge of the canvas, who holds his sword resting on the ground. All Juárez's soldiers were originally presented in a picturesque 'Mexican guerrilla' costume. The firing squad wore red trousers, which were partly overpainted,[51] and their sombreros are seen to be in a process of transformation into képis, so that their costume is on its way to resembling a European uniform, although the two officers on the right are still in Mexican dress.

Manet's repainting of such details on the Boston canvas is assumed to have begun in response to later accounts of the execution, which appeared from 15th July onwards. Since he probably spent part of the summer on the Normandy coast, returning to Paris to attend Baudelaire's funeral on 2nd September, it is unclear just when he started and how long he continued reworking the Boston painting. At some point, he apparently decided he would have to make a fresh start, and abandoned the first version in a provisional and unresolved state. He then sketched out a new design on a second, even larger canvas.

The Second Version: London

It has generally been suggested that Manet started his painting afresh in order to take account of the fuller and more detailed reports of the execution that reached Europe during July and early August, which may, as we have seen, have led to his changing the soldiers' uniforms in the Boston picture (**31** and **31a**, Figs. 57, 58). However, since he never varied his fundamental composition design and never included many of the details that featured in newspaper accounts from the very beginning, we should perhaps look elsewhere for the reason.

60

60. **32**. *The execution of Maximilian*. Second version. 1867–68. Photograph by Lochard, No. 309, c.1883, showing the canvas still largely intact (see Fig. 61). (Bibliothèque Nationale, Cabinet des Estampes, Paris.)

61. *The execution of Maximilian*. Second version (four fragments). 1867–68. 190 by 216 cm. (combined). (The National Gallery, London.)

As he worked on the large Boston canvas, perhaps intending to exhibit it as an instant piece of contemporary reportage (see note 44), Manet must have realised that he had the makings of a great history painting for the Salon, and decided to recast his composition in a more solemn and heroic vein.

The first, Boston, canvas is nearly two metres high by over two-and-a-half wide. The second version, in London – severely damaged and already lacking a wide strip on the left when it was discovered in Manet's studio – must have measured about three metres in width. It was conceived as a broad, frieze-like composition, in which the figures were set out in clearly detached, rhythmically articulated groups, giving it an impressive monumentality.

The evidence of the Lochard photograph

The most complete view of the London painting is the photograph taken by Lochard in Manet's studio in 1883 (**32**, Fig. 60), in which the left part of the canvas has already been trimmed away, so that no more than the Emperor's hand is visible, grasping that of General Miramón.[52] After that, the canvas was apparently rolled up and stored. It suffered further damage and was cut up by Léon, who kept the main, central area and three fragments. These were later reunited by Degas, and still present a very impressive image today (Fig. 61).

In this restatement of the composition in the London picture (**32**, Fig. 60), Manet clarified every aspect of the scene. He reportedly used a photograph for the head of the Emperor, a violinist friend for Miramón and a professional model for the Indian general, Mejía, while an actual squadron of soldiers supplied by his old friend the commandant Lejosne posed in his studio for the executioners.[53] Assuming that Manet began this new version after his return to Paris, in September, he would have had a number of new elements to take into account, and it may well have been these that first led him to rework the Boston painting, before abandoning it.

New information concerning the execution

Some reports published in the second half of July alleged that the generals were shot as traitors, in the back, but this assertion was contradicted by other statements; similarly, there was disagreement about the positions of the condemned men, with the Emperor described as being in the centre or on the right. In the 31st July report, reprinted on 10th August, it was stated that he was allowed to hold the hands of his generals (who were placed with their backs to the firing squads).

Two reports noted the Emperor's reference to the beautiful clear sky; the smart appearance of all three men was commented on, the fact that all of them were wearing civilian dress and that the Emperor was in black. The most direct evidence concerning the soldiers was provided by Albert Wolff, the art critic with whom Manet clashed on more than one occasion. In *Le Figaro* on 11th August, Wolff published the text of a letter and described four photographs received from Mexico. Two of the photographs showed Maximilian's frock-coat and bullet-torn waistcoat, and two purported to show the Emperor's firing squad (see Fig.63).[54]

Wolff's description of the photographs (which Manet could well have asked to see) provided the vital information concerning the appearance of the Mexican soldiers, and no doubt led to Manet's use of French soldiers as models. It also enabled Manet to capitalise on an objective description of the soldiers' appearance in relation to the political and critical content of the work. In describing the photographs, Wolff wrote as follows: '. . . the detachment detailed to execute the Emperor . . . consists of six soldiers, a corporal and an officer. The soldiers' faces are hideous and sinister. Their uniform looks like the French uniform: the képi and jacket appear to be of grey cloth, the belt of white leather; the trousers, which go right down to the feet, are of darker material. The corporal, the one who dealt the death blow to Maximilian, is a handsome young fellow; he has a nice, cheery look about him that is in striking contrast to the lugubrious task he was given. The most bizarre of the seven (*sic*) is the officer commanding the detachment; he looks under eighteen.'[55]

The letter published with Wolff's description of the photographs gave gruesome details of Maximilian's death. He was not killed instantly by the firing squad and several attempts were made to end his agony. Reports of this terrible end were given in several accounts, published on and after 22nd July, the most reliable being one of the latest (and most moving), based on the eye-witness account of Maximilian's cook, published on 10th October.[56] Such details were not relevant to Manet's preoccupations and find no reflection in any of the paintings, but they must have served to reinforce the impression, universally acknowledged, of Maximilian's great courage in the face of death and of the tragic and horrific nature of the execution.

The revised composition

Although there is no way of knowing precisely how the missing Emperor and General Mejía looked on the left of the newly projected painting (**32**, Fig.60), it is clear that Manet was intending to create a documentary picture, based to some extent on authentic, reported information, and on real figures posed in the studio, but organised into a very grand design, suitable for a Salon painting. The setting is summary – an expanse of ground on which the shadows of the figures fall in sharply cut-out shapes, suggesting the sun rising on the high, bare plateau of the Cerro de Campañas. Over the rim of the hill is a far prospect with the suggestion of a range of hills in the blue distance. If the cemetery wall appeared, it must have been in the lost portion of the canvas.

The soldiers in the firing squad, now clearly six in number (see Fig.63), are in virtually the same positions as those in the Boston picture (**31**, Fig.57), but the

62. *Soldier loading his gun.* 1867–68. Pen and sepia ink on tracing paper (laid on card). 26.6 by 9.8 cm. (Michel de Geofroy, Geneva.)

63. Photograph of Maximilian's firing squad.
19th June 1867. See Brown University
exh. cat. [1981], No.28.

figure closest to the victims has been detached from the other five. The handsome
young N.C.O. loading his rifle, evidently painted from a model, is now placed to
the right, more or less combining the positions and poses of the two figures in the
earlier version. A pen and ink outline tracing corresponds very closely to this
figure and was probably used by Manet in the complex process of transferring
elements of his design from one canvas to another (Fig.62). The presence of the
juvenile commanding officer described by Wolff is indicated only by the raised
sword in the background and a hint of his red hat behind the black képis of the
soldiers.

The 'portrait' effect of the N.C.O. is also apparent in the head of General
Miramón, with his regular features and alert expression. However, since Miramón
was posed by Damourette, his appearance does not accord with the description, in
a mid-July account, of his fine beard and brown moustache, or with the photographic likeness that Manet may have seen at a later stage (Fig.66).[57] The clasped
left hands of Miramón and the Emperor are firmly drawn and modelled, and head
and hands are clearly defined, above and below the smoke that was to engulf them
temporarily.

It was in the 31st July account in *L'Indépendance Belge*, reprinted in *Le Mémorial
Diplomatique* on 10th August, that the holding of hands was first reported, although the two generals were there said to have stood with their backs to the
firing squad. Also in that account, a detailed description of the Emperor's appearance was given, and since it partly corresponds with the very sketchy Boston
version of the composition (31, Fig.57), it seems likely that it was also followed in
the second: 'The Emperor, taller than [the generals], rose above them both. He
was dressed in black from head to foot . . . a Mexican hat with its broad brim left
down shaded his head.' (See Fig.65.)

In comparison with the first, Boston version, the victims were evidently brought
closer to the foreground in the London picture, almost in line with the soldiers
(Miramón's head and feet being level with those of the soldier whose head hides
the sword handle). The X-ray evidence of the later Copenhagen sketch (33, Fig.67),
suggests that Mejía, on the far left, was still in virtually the same pose as in the
Boston picture. Manet thus achieved an impressive, frieze-like effect, with two
principal groups of figures and the partly detached N.C.O. set against the bare
ground and blue sky, articulated by the distant horizon at waist-level.

Despite the far greater clarity of the design and the impressively solid, natural
appearance of the figures, the surviving fragments of the London version suggest
that Manet had problems with the scale and relationship of the two groups of

64

65

66

64. Photograph of General Tomás Mejía.
   c.1864–67. See Brown University
   exh. cat. [1981], No.20.
65. Photograph of the Emperor Maximilian.
   1867. See Brown University exh. cat.
   [1981], No.19.
66. Photograph of General Miguel Miramón.
   c.1864–67. See Brown University exh. cat.
   [1981], No.21.

figures. Miramón certainly appears too large in relation to the soldiers. Whatever the reasons, after two full-scale attempts, Manet apparently felt the need to rethink his composition on a smaller scale, and everything indicates that the oil sketch in Copenhagen was painted next in the sequence.

An Intermediate Design:
The Copenhagen X-ray and the lithograph

The visible surface of the small and vividly painted oil sketch in Copenhagen (**35**, Fig.69, Col.ill.10) has a dramatic quality that is immediately striking. As already indicated, it shows clear signs of overpainting, and X-radiography has revealed the underlying composition, which relates it very clearly back to the first and second versions (**31** and **32**, Figs.57, 60/61) and on to the final painting in Mannheim (**37**, Fig.71, Col.ill.11). Its status as a 'working sketch' is also emphasised by the grid lines that indicate two separate squaring-up operations, one under and one over the second, repainted state of this little picture.[58]

The Copenhagen X-ray evidence

The X-radiograph of the Copenhagen oil sketch (**33**, Fig.67)[59] reveals the substantial changes made by Manet, in two stages, to this composition. The X-ray image shows the group of victims, which was apparently too large and out of scale in the London painting, reduced in size and brought much closer to the group of soldiers. This change brings the revised composition closer to the first, Boston painting (**30**, Fig.57).

The Copenhagen X-ray image shows both changes and similarities in relation to the Boston picture. On the left, General Mejía stands in much the same position as in the Boston version, with head bowed and a stance that appears to be half way between that in the Boston and final Copenhagen versions (see **30** and **35**, Figs.57 and 69). Maximilian is virtually identical with the image in the Boston painting and his sombrero and beard are sketched-in in much the same way. Even in the ghostly form of the X-ray image, his appearance is strikingly close to a photograph

67. **33.** *The execution of Maximilian.* Intermediate design. 1868. Positive print from a composite X-radiograph of No.35 (Fig.69).

68. **34.** *The execution of Maximilian.* 1868. Lithograph. 33.3 by 43.3 cm. Edition of 1884. (The British Museum, London.)

that shows him wearing his Mexican sombrero (Fig.65).[60] Because he has been moved down in relation to the soldiers, the smoke now billows below, rather than above the gun barrels, since it would otherwise have obscured his face.

Compared with the London picture (**32**, Figs.60/61), the group of victims has been brought so close to the soldiers that Miramón's left arm, with its full, white shirtsleeve gathered into a wide cuff, now appears behind that of the soldier nearest the victims, and his left leg meets the soldier's just above the white spat. The most notable change in the group of soldiers is the emergence into full view of the young commanding officer. With his sword raised high (having presumably,

69. 35. Sketch for *The execution of Maximilian*. 1868–69/1879? 50 by 60 cm. (Ny Carlsberg Glyptotek, Copenhagen.) Col. ill. 10.

as in the London version, given the command to fire by raising rather than lowering his sword), he is placed behind the front line of soldiers (an impossible position from which to give a sword command) and does not quite fill the space between the rear soldier and the N.C.O. loading his gun.

As to the setting, the X-ray image is not easy to interpret, but there appears to be a light-toned wall behind the figures, with trees above, in other words, a corner of the cemetery that features in the final Mannheim version (37, Fig. 71, Col. ill. 11). It is not clear where the wall ends, but the lithograph (34, Fig. 68) suggests several possible readings of the X-ray image.

The lithograph

The image most closely related to the Copenhagen X-ray is the lithograph (34, Fig. 68) on which Manet must have been working at the same time as he was revising his composition in the oil sketch. In the lithograph, as in the Copenhagen X-ray, Maximilian wears a horizontally placed sombrero, smoke billows over his chest, and the victims' legs and feet are in the same positions.

Although the wall in the lithograph is broadly similar to the wall in the final state of the Copenhagen sketch (35, Fig. 69, Col. ill. 10), in that it runs behind all the figures, up to the right edge of the composition, there are also significant differences. Comparison with the Copenhagen X-ray helps to clarify the reworking visible in both the lithograph and the oil sketch.

On the left of the lithograph, the wall appears to show two different base lines, the 'final' one at some distance behind the figures, running diagonally back towards the far wall against which the soldiers are silhouetted; and a first, nearer base line which has been merged by scraping into the lighter ground tone, but seems to have passed originally behind Mejía's outstretched legs (and even to have been visible between his left and Maximilian's right leg).

As finally shown in the lithograph, the base line of the wall could never meet the angle of the wall, seen above the central soldier, where it ostensibly changes plane. Furthermore, the wall behind the soldiers actually continues past the angle at its base and is still running horizontally where it is glimpsed between the soldier and General Miramón. The evidence of these shifts in the placing of the wall in the lithograph serve to clarify a reading of the Copenhagen X-ray image.

In the X-ray (33, Fig. 67), the victims appear to be standing with their backs close to a wall whose base runs back in a diagonal, perspective line and is visible between Mejía's legs. This position of the wall was followed initially in the lithograph, and both oil sketch and lithograph may then have been altered to push the base of the wall farther away. Its upper and right edges, seen in the X-ray, were probably also followed in the lithograph (34, Fig. 68) and then modified (there are clear signs of rework) when Manet decided to extend the wall. In the lithograph, it becomes not the exterior wall of a cemetery but, through the change of plane, the interior wall of a courtyard.

The setting of the victims against the wall in the Copenhagen X-ray image (33, Fig. 67) was not unlike Goya's placing of his victims, on a diagonal plane, against a low hill, in the *Third of May* composition (see Fig. 59). In the X-ray of the oil sketch, the wall shows light. In the black-and-white medium of the lithograph, where Manet needed a foil to set off the victims' heads, the wall is dark. This may explain why he preserved the perspective view of the left wall and the distant placing of the wall behind the soldiers. In the lithograph, the dark base line of the wall behind the soldiers lies on a level with the soldiers' white belts, and serves to underline the rhythms of the grouping across the composition. The lighter ground below the wall accentuates the dramatic patterning of both soldiers' and victims' legs, with the sharp accents of the white spats and conflicting movements of shadows and feet.

Oil sketch and lithograph seem, therefore, to have developed simultaneously. In the sketch, Manet made the radical alteration that changes the perspective view of the cemetery wall on the left (33, Fig. 67) into a continuous flat backdrop for his frieze of figures (35, Fig. 69, Col. ill. 10). He did not adopt this final solution in the lithograph, perhaps for primarily pictorial – or rather graphic – reasons.

The lithograph, while sharing many elements of the underlying sketch composition, also shows several of its final features (see 35, Fig. 69, Col. ill. 10): the throwing back of Mejía's head, and the broadening of the outline of the commanding officer so that his left arm touches the N.C.O.'s right shoulder, leaving no space between the figures. It seems unlikely, from what we know of his normal practice, that Manet would have made an oil sketch in preparation for a lithograph, and more probable that he intended the lithograph to reproduce his Salon painting. One must therefore assume that oil sketch and lithograph were in progress at the same time and that the final Mannheim version of his composition (37, Fig. 71, Col. ill. 11) grew out of further modifications made to the oil sketch after the lithograph was virtually complete.

The Final Design: Copenhagen (final state) and Mannheim

Having returned, after the second, London version of the composition (32, Figs. 60/61), to a closer grouping of the figures in the initial Copenhagen sketch composition (33, Fig. 67), Manet was again faced by problems of scale and of the effectiveness of his dramatic narrative. In moving closer to the firing squad, the victims lost their stature, both literally and figuratively, and were overpowered by the soldiers. In the Copenhagen X-ray and the lithograph (33 and 34, Figs. 67, 68), all the heads are virtually on the same level, with the tallest soldier rising higher than the victims, while the victims' legs and feet appear slight and insubstantial in relation to the solid, spatted shoes of the soldiers, rooted to the ground as they fire their heavy muskets.

Final revisions to the Copenhagen sketch

Manet must have been aware of this lack of differentiation in the figures as he worked on the revised sketch composition and completed his lithograph (34, Fig.68). After making the slight adjustments to the position of the wall on the left, which we have already seen, he then made a major change that radically altered the effect of the whole composition of the Copenhagen sketch (35, Fig.69, Col.ill.10) and provided the solution adopted in the third and final canvas (37, Fig.71).

Taking a loaded brush, Manet painted over the legs and feet of the victims and their shadows on the ground, literally pushing the figures up the canvas, and therefore back into the picture space, until they were once again almost separated from the soldiers. They were now placed on a much more dramatic, diagonal plane (emphasised by the extension of Miramón's outflung left leg), to which Manet gave maximum impact by suppressing any anecdotal references to a natural, three-dimensional setting and by painting-in a blank, flat, mid-grey wall, parallel with the picture plane and extending down to a point not far behind Miramón's left foot. Above the wall (which may at some stage have been as high as in the lithograph – see 33 and 34, Figs.67, 68), is a very sketchy indication of the background that was to appear in the Mannheim painting (37, Fig.71).

Manet further increased the dramatic impact of the scene by making several telling alterations to the figures. At a stage early enough to have been followed in the lithograph (34, Fig.68), Mejía's head, previously bowed on his chest (33, Fig.67), was flung back in a pathetic gesture that bares his throat and suggests the terrible impact of the shots in his chest. The Emperor was given added stature and a symbolic affinity with Christ and the idea of martyrdom by the simple expedient of turning up the brim of his rather prosaic sombrero, so that it creates the effect of a halo around his head.

In the course of resolving his sketch composition, Manet must have started to transfer it to his final, large canvas (37, Fig.71, Col.ill.11). There are pencil numbers on the paint surface of the Copenhagen sketch, down the left edge, with a corresponding squaring of the canvas. This ceases to be visible in the more heavily repainted areas on the ground and above the top of the wall (presumably the last areas to be reworked). In addition, pencilled points all round the edges of the canvas suggest that Manet made another grid when the sketch was finally complete, its small intervals reflecting the huge scale of the final painting in relation to the sketch.

The X-ray state of the Mannheim painting

The huge Mannheim canvas, measuring just over two-and-a-half by three metres, is probably the largest of Manet's three full-scale versions of his Maximilian composition (37, Fig.71, Col.ill.11). Following its recent examination and restoration, there is now X-ray evidence (36, Fig.70), to show how Manet arrived at his final result.[61]

When the X-ray image of the Mannheim canvas is compared with the final state of the Copenhagen sketch (35, Fig.69, Col.ill.10), similarities and differences are immediately apparent. The victims are virtually the same, although Maximilian's hat is not pushed so far back on his head and its shape is much more clearly defined.

The central soldier, whose right arm overlaps the soldier to his right in the sketch, now stands as a completely detached figure, balancing the N.C.O. on the right. Most importantly, the commanding officer, placed between the soldiers and the N.C.O. in the Copenhagen sketch, makes a ghostly appearance, in the same position, in the Mannheim X-ray image, first added, and then obliterated in the final state of the canvas (37, Fig.71, Col.ill.11).[62] In the vast Mannheim painting, compared with the relatively tiny oil sketch (35, Fig.69, Col.ill.10), the officer's

70. **36**. *The execution of Maximilian*. Third
version. Positive print from a composite
X-radiograph of No. 37 (Fig. 71).

presence next to the N.C.O. would have been very noticeable, marked by the
raised sword, his red képi and the red trouser leg which appears immediately
below the butt of the N.C.O.'s musket. In the final state of the Mannheim canvas
(**37**, Fig. 71, Col. ill. 11), his presence is suggested by two touches of red behind the
soldiers – an even more subliminal indication than in the London picture (**32**,
Figs. 60/61). As far as one can judge from the Mannheim X-ray image, the wall was
laid-in in the same position, with the spectators, who are only suggested in the
Copenhagen sketch (**35**, Fig. 69, Col. ill. 10), already present though perhaps not
altogether in their final form.

The final Mannheim composition

Apart from the overpainting of the commanding officer, Manet made several
minor but significant adjustments in completing his final Mannheim canvas
(**37**, Fig. 71, Col. ill. 11). Mejía's head was reworked to bring his features into view
and give them a distinctly heroic cast, so that he, like the other two prisoners,
became an individualised victim.[63] Maximilian's features appear to have been
softened in the final retouching, and the clasped hands were altered, blurred and
transformed into a powerful evocation of bloodshed and death. Through further
subtle adjustments, the victims are finally presented as a united but utterly vul-
nerable group – the two generals swaying towards the supporting, column-like
form of the Emperor – as they face the stolid, unmoving forms of the firing squad.

Immediately above the squad, Mexican peasants (already indicated in the lithograph (**34**, Fig. 68)), struggle to look over the wall, while further crowds are massed
on the distant slope. The similarity of the figures to the groups of onlookers
watching the bullfight in Goya's *Tauromaquia* prints has been noted and is surely
significant. Their faces and gestures express horror and dismay, and recall the
account of Maximilian's cook, who described how 'the people openly expressed
their sympathy and indignation', adding that 'No man from the upper classes
showed himself. The crowd was composed principally of poor Indians and ladies

71. **37**. *The execution of Maximilian*. Third version. 1868–69/1879? Signed and dated *19 Juin 1867*. 252 by 305 cm. (Städtische Kunsthalle, Mannheim.) Col. ill. 11.

fearlessly showing where their sympathies lay.' He again referred to popular Indian sympathy expressed by the crowds at the execution: 'Behind the prisoners, higher up the hill, the people were waiting, almost all of them poor Indians.'[64]

In the final state, the officer giving the command is represented only by a glimpse of his red képi and a symbolic thin red line (the tassel of his sword?) against the ground below. His occultation serves to increase the sense of a pre-ordained, autonomous, sacrificial act. The last vestige of anecdotal detail, the last element that might distract from concentration on the execution itself, has finally been removed. Like the soldiers of Napoleon I in Goya's Spain, in 1808 (Fig. 59), the 'French'-uniformed firing squad, inexorably set in motion by Napoleon III's intervention in Mexico, acts out its rôle, faced by the ill-fated Emperor Maximilian whose courage binds him to his two loyal generals, one Spanish-Mexican, the other Indian. A crowd of indigenous Mexican-Indians condemns the barbarous act, and on the surface of the canvas, as if to symbolise his own, thrice-reiterated, involvement, Manet adds his signature and the historic date, as of an eye-witness to the events of 19th June 1867.

The Aftermath

The painting was completed and the lithograph was ready for publication by January 1869. As we now know from many documents,[65] Manet was prevented by 'the authorities' from presenting his works to the public: the lithograph (**34**, Fig. 68) remained unpublished until after his death, and the painting (**37**, Fig. 71, Col. ill. 11) was not submitted to the Salon jury since he was given to understand that it would be refused. Zola openly accused the government of censorship and the affair was aired in the press. In the end, Manet regained possession of his lithographic stone (which the printer, Lemercier, had threatened to efface) and confined his picture to the obscurity of his studio.

In the winter of 1879 the picture was shipped to the United States and exhibited as an individual show piece at the Clarendon Hotel on Broadway, New York, and at the Studio Building Gallery on Ipswich Street, Boston. The two-city tour was organised by Emilie Ambre, a singer whom Manet had just met when he was taking an autumn rest and cure for his ailing legs at Bellevue that same year. The project to show the painting may also have had something to do with Méry Laurent, who was a close friend of both Mallarmé and Manet at this time. Manet gave Méry the Copenhagen oil sketch (35, Fig.69) and she and Emilie probably worked together to persuade the ill and often discouraged artist to exhibit the painting outside France.

Handbills (Fig.72) were printed in English and an explanatory notice (38) announced an *EXHIBITION OF MR. E. MANET'S CELEBRATED PAINTING, "The Execution of the Emperor Maximilian"*. With some errors of date and historical fact, the American public was informed:

On the 15th of June, 1867, at 10 o'clock P.M., a council of war held at Querétaro condemned to death the Emperor Maximilian and the two generals Miramón and Mejía, who had been made prisoners.

On the 18th of June, at 6 A.M., the three prisoners were shot in the "Cero de las Campañas".

In the same year, that final episode of the war between France and Mexico was used as a motive by the celebrated French painter, E. Manet. With his well-known talent as a naturalist, no other could paint such a moving drama in a more truthful manner.

Mr E. Manet knew how to give a striking resemblance to the three victims. Maximilian, in the centre, has on his right General Mejía, on his left General Miramón; the Sergeant behind the platoon of executioners is preparing his gun for the finishing stroke.

This picture was considered in France as being so startling, that its exhibition was formally prohibited; therefore but few of Mr E. Manet's friends have been enabled to see and admire it in his studio in Paris.

This document[66] expressly states that the painting shown in America was the one whose exhibition was 'formally prohibited' in France. The question that remains is whether the final alterations made to the large painting were carried out before January 1869, or at some later date, possibly before the picture was despatched to America, and whether any of the alterations to the Copenhagen sketch (35, Fig.69, Col.ill.10) were similarly carried out, after the prohibition of both painting and lithograph. It still seems strange that Manet should have planned to publish a lithograph that was strikingly different from the painting he intended to exhibit at the Salon, and the suppression of the commanding officer in the Mannheim painting, at least, may have occurred at a later date than has hitherto been suspected.

72. Handbill announcing the exhibition of the *Execution of Maximilian* (third version, see No. 37, Fig.71) at 757 Broadway, New York, in the winter of 1879–1880. (Private collection.)

'La Barricade': The project and the lithograph

Although Manet was prevented from showing his painting or publishing his lithograph of the *Execution of Maximilian* (34 and 37, Figs.68, 71), he did not altogether abandon his great composition. After the Franco-Prussian war and the siege of Paris (during which he served, like Degas, in the National Guard), Manet left Paris in February 1871, returning with his family immediately after the final blood bath of the *semaine sanglante* that put an end to the Commune. Whether or not he was an eye-witness of the events, here, once again, was a heroic subject for a grand contemporary history painting that Manet seems to have planned but never executed.

There exists a large double-sided drawing (39, Figs.73, 74) that shows on one side a reversed tracing from the 'Maximilian' lithograph (34 and 39v, Figs.68, 74), and on the other a scene of the summary execution of Communards by government troops in front of a barricade (39r, Fig.73). The traced image (39v, Fig.74) was indented on a sheet of strong paper that ends above the heads of the figures, and

73. **39** (recto). *La barricade*. 1867–68?/1871. Brush and Indian ink, watercolour and gouache over pencil, on two joined sheets of paper (wove lower half, laid upper half). 46.4 by 32.6 cm. (Szépmüvészeti Múzeum, Budapest.)

74. **39** (verso). *The execution of Maximilian* (reversed composition). 1867–68/1871? Indented lines, partially redrawn with black chalk, on strong wove paper. 30.5 by 32.6 cm. (before the addition of the upper sheet). See No. **39** recto (Fig. 73).

the outlines of the central soldier and the victims have been marked with black chalk. On the other side of the sheet (**39r**, Fig. 73), the contours of the 'Maximilian' composition are still visible in pencil, but have been radically transformed with brush and wash, water-colour and gouache, to turn Maximilian and his generals into a group of Communards, and the Mexican firing squad into French government forces.

It is not possible at present to tell whether this lower sheet was originally drawn in preparation for one of the 'Maximilian' versions, or was made specifically to give Manet's prohibited composition a new lease of life, in a new context, as a painting on the theme of the Paris Commune. One detail which suggests that it may have served in the development of the 'Maximilian' composition is the bowed head of the 'Mejía' communard. This corresponds with the X-ray image underlying the Copenhagen sketch (**33**, Fig. 67), and could suggest either the use of this drawing for one of the earlier 'Maximilian' compositions, or the possibility, mentioned above, that some of the final alterations to the Copenhagen and Mannheim pictures were not carried out until later, in fact until after 1871.

To the horizontal 'Maximilian' design, Manet added another sheet of paper to give the composition an upright format (**39r**, Fig. 73). The Emperor and the Mexicans – betrayed generals shot by their own people – were transformed into French citizens – liberal 'rebels' and government soldiers – and a Parisian street scene was added to complete the setting, with the barricade and an overturned barrel in the foreground.

If this new design was intended as a study for a Salon painting,[67] either Manet did not have the courage and energy to carry it through, or he again met with official hostility. He reproduced the composition on a smaller scale, in a lithograph which, like the *Execution of Maximilian*, was not published until after his death

(**40**, Fig. 75). The only work on this theme that he succeeded in publishing during his life-time was the lithograph entitled *Guerre civile*, printed by Lemercier and issued in 1874 (**41**, Fig. 76), in which the dead and unidentified victim offers no threat to public order.

75. **40**. *La barricade*. c.1871. Lithograph. 46.5 by 33.4 cm. First state. Possibly a contemporary impression, before the edition of 1884. (Szépmüvészeti Múzeum, Budapest.)

76. **41**. *Guerre civile*. 1871–73. Signed and dated 1871. Lithograph. 39.9 by 58 cm. Edition of 1874. (British Museum, London.)

Cafés-Concerts
and the Folies-Bergère

The post-war years

After the Franco-Prussian war, the siege of Paris and the terrible days of the Commune, there is a visible change in the themes and tenor of Manet's painting; and the depression from which he was reported to suffer after the events of the war and the Commune must have been relieved in part by his meeting with the dealer Durand-Ruel, who in January 1872 bought an important group of works – twenty-four in all – from his studio.[68]

At the outbreak of the war, Manet had given up his studio on the rue Guyot, in a rather isolated, western area of Paris. From 1870, his studios as well as his homes were near the Place Clichy and the Place Pigalle,[69] and in July 1872, perhaps as a direct result of the sale to Durand-Ruel, he took a magnificent studio (a former fencing hall),[70] in the rue de St Pétersbourg, the street in which he was then living, with views over the rue Mosnier and the Pont de l'Europe, and across the railway lines to the gardens on the rue de Rome.

The Nouvelle-Athènes café on the Place Pigalle had by then become the most fashionable meeting-place for artists and writers. And café scenes, or scenes of public places of entertainment generally, began to appear in Manet's work from this time. Between 1872 and his death in 1883, Manet executed a large number of paintings and pastels showing the interiors or terraces or gardens of the popular brasseries, restaurants, cafés and café-concerts of the day.

Manet's café series 1877–1882

In February 1874, a print by Manet was proofed, if not actually published (Fig.78).[71] It shows the interior of a café, with a waiter standing near a group of men drinking at a table, and figures at the billiard tables in an adjoining room. Manet chose a similar scene as the basis of a major painting project on which he worked in the late 1870s. Its subsequent transformations, through canvases cut, rejoined and reworked, and compositions started afresh – very much as in the 'Maximilian' series (see pp.48–64), or even the *Nymphe surprise – Déjeuner sur l'herbe* sequence of many years before (see pp.26–47) – led ultimately to the painting of his final masterpiece, *A bar at the Folies-Bergère* (**62**, Fig.104, Col.ill.9), which was shown at the Salon of 1882, just a year before his death. The story is a very complex one, but from the mass of evidence now available,[72] it can be summarised as follows.

Reichshoffen – The painting and the place

Two pictures, in Winterthur and London (**45** and **46**, Figs.81, 82, Col.ills.4, 5), were originally painted by Manet on a single, large canvas. We now know that the right edge of the Winterthur canvas once joined the left edge of the London canvas without a break: the fingertips, on the London canvas, of the girl in profile on the Winterthur canvas, are there to prove it, and there are many pieces of evidence that help to show what the original large painting looked like (**42**, Fig.78).

It showed a group of the artist's friends at a café table, with a large window in the background. Léon Leenhoff and Manet's friends and early biographers identified the setting as the Brasserie Reichshoffen on the Boulevard Rochechouart, and also named several of the figures in the scene; on the left (now in the Winterthur picture), the actress Ellen Andrée and the young engraver Henri Guérard; on the right (in the London picture), according to Léon, a glimpse of another young artist, Norbert Goeneutte, and 'Manet's grey hat', as well as the brasserie waitress.

All efforts to identify the Brasserie Reichshoffen have so far failed and no trace has yet been found of such an establishment on the Boulevard Rochechouart.[73] It is, however, indicated as the scene of Manet's painting in Léon's register of Manet's works and through his annotations on a Lochard photograph of the London picture

77. **42**. *Reichshoffen*. 1877–78. Diagrammatic reconstruction of the large painting, showing the three cutting points (1, 2, 3) and the possible extent of the original design based on a combination of the two existing canvases (a – 3) and (3 – c) and a drawing (b – d). See Nos.**43**, **45** and **46** (Figs.79, 81 and 82).

78

79

78. *Le café. Interior of the Café Guerbois?* 1874. Transfer pen lithograph. 26.3 by 33.4 cm. (Private collection.)

79. **43.** *Café scene.* c.1877. Pencil on a double page of a squared notebook, with manuscript annotations *blanc* and *rouge*. 14.2 by 18.7 cm. (Musée du Louvre, Cabinet des Dessins, Paris.)

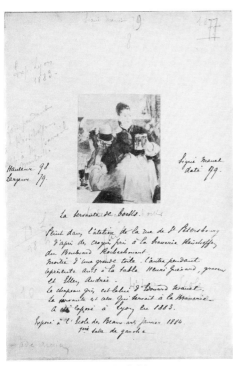

80. **44.** *'La servante de bocks'* (see No. **46**, Fig. **82**). Photograph by Lochard, No. 8, mounted on card, with annotations by Léon Leenhoff. 1883. 9.1 by 5.9 cm. (photograph), 29 by 20 cm. (card). (Bibliothèque Nationale, Cabinet des Estampes, Paris.)

(**44**, Fig. 80). Léon recorded that the London canvas was half of a picture – the other half being in Marseille – that Manet painted in his studio on the rue de St Pétersbourg from sketches made in the Brasserie Reichshoffen, and that the figures represented were those indicated above.[74]

Léon's indications make it clear that the large painting was executed in Manet's studio on the rue de St Pétersbourg,[75] and suggest that it may have been under way in 1877. While describing the London picture for his register of the contents of Manet's studio after the artist's death, Léon was also recording what he knew about the painting of the large canvas and its subsequent dismemberment, just a few years earlier.[76]

The 'Reichshoffen' composition

We do not have an entirely clear idea of what the large painting looked like before Manet cut and altered it. (This is discussed in more detail below.) It does, however, appear that the canvas, apparently composed on an impressive scale, showed figures drinking at a long table in front of a large café window, to which, behind a net curtain, a poster was affixed. Although the poster was to be read from the the pavement outside, and the lettering appears in reverse, one can clearly make out the name *Hanlon Lees*, printed along the bottom edge. The Hanlon Lees brothers were a team of American trapeze artists whose act, with Little Bob, was one of the principal attractions at the Folies-Bergère from at least as early as 1872 (**58**, Fig. 100).[77]

The cast of characters and their setting

On either side of the marble table, Manet portrayed some of the long-suffering friends who would consent to sit for him. And it must surely be significant that Ellen Andrée, who posed for Degas's *Absinthe* in 1876 but fled after a few sittings as Manet's model in *Chez le Père Lathuille* (Fig. 13) – shown at the Salon of 1880 – is no more than sketched in on the bare, primed canvas (on the Winterthur picture, **45**, Fig. 81, Col. ill. 4), whereas Guérard beside her, the figures across the table, and above all the head of the unknown girl in profile, were obviously worked and reworked in the course of many sessions.[78]

Beyond the vivacious actress boldly engaging the viewer through the picture frame, Henri Guérard cuts an elegant figure with top hat, handle-bar moustache and neatly trimmed beard. Guérard was a gifted young etcher who met Manet towards 1877, when he would have been just over thirty. He was soon helping with the technical side of Manet's print-making, and in 1879 married Eva Gonzalès, who had become Manet's pupil a decade earlier.[79] Guérard seems to be in active conversation with the friends on the other side of the table, but this is where certainty breaks down, since we cannot be sure that the reworked figures on the London canvas are as Manet originally portrayed them (**46**, Fig. 82, Col. ill. 5).

If, as Léon recorded, one of the London figures is the painter Norbet Goeneutte, he would then have been a young man of about twenty-three. He was a painter-etcher and friend of the Impressionists – in 1876 he posed for Renoir in the *Moulin de la Galette* and *The swing* – and was described and depicted[80] as a 'dandy de la bohème'. So it seems unlikely that he could be the man in the blue smock (whose features appear little changed in the X-ray image). And if he, rather than Manet, was wearing 'Manet's grey hat', as Léon referred to it, his profile was later obscured by the blue-smocked man's hand and pipe.[81]

Théodore Duret, the friend to whom Manet handed his most valuable paintings for safe-keeping during the siege of Paris, recorded that the man in the foreground was the waitress's protector, who accompanied her while she posed in the artist's studio.[82] The X-ray images of the London picture and its Paris variant (**47** and **48**, Figs. 83, 84),[83] suggest that the waitress originally looked out of the canvas, with a smile on her parted lips. As the men talked across the table, the two women were

81. **45.** *Au café.* Signed and dated 1878. 77 by
 83 cm. (Sammlung Oskar Reinhart 'Am
 Römerholz', Winterthur.) Col. ill. 4.
82. **46.** *Coin de café-concert (The waitress).*
 1877–79. Signed and dated 1878 (or 1879).
 98 by 79 cm. (The National Gallery,
 London.) Col. ill. 5.

thus drawing the viewer into the conversation with their sympathetic glances, and Manet evidently established a strongly balanced group of figures around the dynamic, receding lines of the table, with the Hanlon Lees poster on the large, flat surface of the window to help reaffirm the flatness of the picture plane.

Manet must have intended this bold, attractive subject from modern life as his own, indoor version of paintings like Renoir's *Moulin de la Galette*, and it was clearly – in its original scale – a Salon picture. If Léon was right, and the picture was composed in 1877, it was probably painted with the following Salon in mind. However, 1878 was the year of another Exposition Universelle. Once again, as in 1867 (see p. 46), Manet decided not to risk the indignity of having some or all of his pictures rejected. He therefore submitted nothing and made vague plans to open his studio to the public, as he had done on an earlier occasion. In the end, he took no action. And it may have been after this decision that he abandoned the idea of *Reichshoffen* as a Salon picture, felt dissatisfied, and cast about for ways of reworking his design. By July 1878, he had moved into Rosen's studio. In 1879, he sold first one and then another canvas, cut from the *Reichshoffen* composition.

'Reichshoffen' cut and sold twice over

In Manet's account book for the years from 1872 until his death, are the entries for the sale of both pictures derived from the *Reichshoffen* composition. Sales of paintings for the year 1879 include: 'Reischoffen [*sic*] (Baroille de Marseille) 1500 fr', followed three lines later by 'Un coin de café (Barroille Marseille) 2500 fr' [*sic*].[84] Tabarant purported to explain the successive sales of the paintings: M. Etienne Barroil (a gentleman from Marseille introduced to Manet by Méry Laurent, according to Proust) acquired the right (London) picture and then, because his wife did not like it, returned it to Manet, presumably in part exchange for the more expensive left half (Winterthur).[85]

83

83. **47**. *Coin de café-concert*. Positive print from a composite X-radiograph of No.**46** (Fig.82), showing part of the original *Reichshoffen* composition with the right side of the window seen in No.**45** (Fig.81).

84. **48**. *La serveuse de bocks*. Positive print from a composite X-radiograph of No.**49** (Fig.85), showing the same area of window as in No.**47** (Fig.83).

85. **49**. *La serveuse de bocks*. c.1878–80. 77.5 by 65 cm. (Musée d'Orsay – Galeries du Jeu de Paume, Paris.) Col.ill.7.

84

85

To the picture M. Barroil first acquired (**46**, Fig. 82, Col. ill. 5), Manet gave the title of his original composition, *Reichshoffen*, in his account book (calling it *Coin de café-concert* in the catalogue of the 1880 Vie Moderne exhibition, when it had been extensively repainted); the second picture sold to Barroil he entitled *Un coin de café* (**45**, Fig. 81, Col. ill. 4), according to the same account book. The Winterthur picture was therefore complete, as we see it now, with any rework, its signature and its 1878 date, by the time M. Barroil took it in place of the London canvas.

It is very probable that the London picture corresponded at that time with the style and finish of the Winterthur picture and was therefore still at an intermediate stage, and almost certainly without the café-concert motifs in the background.[86]

The cut canvas – 'Reichshoffen' before and after *

A diagrammatic reconstruction (**42**, Fig. 77) gives an idea of the relationship of the two parts of the original *Reichshoffen* picture, and also shows the line (1), on the Winterthur side, along which Manet first divided his canvas, rejoining and re-painting it when he decided the new format was not to his liking. In the diagram, the two sections cut from the *Reichshoffen* canvas are combined with a drawing (**43**, Fig. 79) which almost certainly provided the basis for Manet's composition.

The drawing (**43**, Fig. 79) is a very quick pencil sketch, made on a double page of small, squared notebook of the sort that Manet constantly carried with him.[87] The drawing suggests the possible limits of a much larger composition and the reconstruction (**42**, Fig. 77) shows how Manet may have approached the problem of establishing one or more new compositions from the original *Reichshoffen* design.

The first cut (1) would have produced a fragment on the extreme left, consisting of a striking figure group.[88] The right-hand piece of canvas left Manet with the possibility of creating a balanced composition, still with figures on either side of the table, in a canvas extending from a left edge at (1) to an unknown right edge some-where between (c – d) and (2), the point at which he decided to make another cut.

The girl in profile in the Winterthur canvas, who appears so large and out of scale in that picture as we see it today, may have been added at this point, to provide the necessary counterweight to the 'London' figures (probably already two or more) on the right. Manet would then have made his second cut (2) to establish the right edge of his new design. He seems to have cut through the existing composition, and not simply trimmed his original canvas at the right edge; for the X-ray image of the London picture (**47**, Fig. 83) shows that the waitress was originally placed farther to the right and that the cut passed through her shoulder and along the side of her face in its original position.[89]

The fact that he moved the waitress and repainted her farther from the cut right edge supports the view that Manet wanted to reintegrate her into the new com-position, whose side edges were to be cuts (1) and (2) in the original canvas. At this stage, therefore, Manet was apparently still using only the original *Reichshoffen* canvas, and the wide strip that he later joined to the right of the London section (2 – c) had not yet been added. In order to find a new and satisfactory relationship between the seated figures and the waitress whom he wished to move closer to them, Manet sketched his composition again on a fresh canvas, now in Paris.

The Paris canvas *

The Paris canvas (**49**, Fig. 85, Col. ill. 7) has been cut on three sides and only the right edge is the original one, showing bare, primed canvas tacked to the stretcher.[90] The X-ray image of the Paris canvas (**48**, Fig. 84) shows, like the London one (**47**, Fig. 83), a light area corresponding to the right side of the *Reichshoffen* café window, and an underlying paint layer that continues round the left edge of the stretcher appears closely related to the original composition. It therefore seems very likely that the Paris canvas was once the same size as the canvas Manet originally cut

*See pp. 84–85.

from his large *Reichshoffen* composition, with its left edge at (1) on the reconstruction (**42**, Fig. 77), and that it was reduced in size only after Manet had decided to find new formats for his *Reichshoffen* fragments.

When Manet decided to reattach the girl in profile to the left-hand section of canvas, he cut the canvas yet again, through the centre of the table (3). This formed the picture M. Barroil finally acquired (section a–3, the canvas now in Winterthur), but it left Manet with a tall, narrow piece of canvas and an ill-balanced composition (3–2). It must have been at this stage that he added a wide strip of canvas to the right edge and extended the figures and background over it. However, Manet was still in his 'café', rather than his 'café-concert' phase, and the painting added on the new strip (2–c) did not yet include the stage curtain and the double bass player. The concert was still to come.[91]

From brasserie to café-concert

So far, the distinctive addition of the various café-concert motifs to all three pictures has only been touched on. It must be significant that at the very end of the 1870s Manet should have turned from café and brasserie scenes – *Reichshoffen*, *La prune*, *Le bouchon* and an unidentified picture entitled *Assommoir* (in the account book in which he noted its sale to Faure in 1877)[92] – to the café-concert and, finally, to that palace of Parisian entertainment, the Folies-Bergère.

The three canvases to which Manet specifically gave 'café-concert' titles – the right-hand fragment of the former *Reichshoffen* picture in London (and by extension its Paris variant), and the little Baltimore painting (**54**, Fig. 94, Col. ill. 6) – were transformed by the addition of direct or mirrored views of a stage with performers: in the London picture, a ballet dancer; in the Paris variant, a singer in a white dress; in the Baltimore picture the recognisable figure of Elsa la Polonaise, of whom there is also a print (**52**, Fig. 92).

Léon Leenhoff described the *Reichshoffen* composition as having been painted from sketches made in the brasserie on the Boulevard Rochechouart, of which

86. **50**. *At the café-concert*. c.1878–80. Pencil with black chalk corrections on a double page from a squared notebook. 13.1 by 16.6 cm. (Musée du Louvre, Cabinet des Dessins, Paris.)

87. *At the café-concert*. c.1878–80. Brush and ink wash over pencil, on transparent paper (laid down). 21.7 by 28 cm. (Musée du Louvre, Cabinet des Dessins, Paris.)

only one appears to have survived (**43**, Fig. 79). All the concert motifs later incorporated into the pictures derived from the *Reichshoffen* composition are found in drawings – either quick notations on sketchbook pages, or redrawn from these in ink, to serve as the basis for prints and reproductions. In the London picture, there is also a glimpse of the orchestra, first captured in pencil on the double page of a small notebook (**50**, Fig. 86) and then redrawn in ink wash on the kind of semi-transparent paper that was used for transfer prints (Fig. 87).[93] This type of 'croquis' (**50**, Fig. 86) demonstrates how Manet made use of the most summary notations, to create further drawings or to provide very precise motifs for paintings, in this case the background of the London *Coin de café-concert* (**46**, Fig. 82, Col. ill. 5). He also sketched the same musicians, this time in a larger notebook and with the conductor's music stand and baton clearly visible on the left and a male singer on stage (**51**, Fig. 88),[94] while another double page pencil sketch, probably from the same notebook, shows part of the audience and the lower half of a woman performer on stage (Fig. 89).

Sketching at the café-concert on the Champs-Elysées

Two drawings in Léon Leenhoff's register of Manet's works are described under Nos. 187 and 188 as *Chanteuse profil droite* and *Chanteuse prof[il] gauche*. They both appear in the Lochard photograph albums with annotations describing them as sketches of a café-concert singer on the Champs-Elysées, made on yellow paper (Figs. 90, 91).[95] The drawing of the singer in profile to the left appears almost identical with the print of *La belle Polonaise* (**52**, Fig. 92)[96] and shows the performer on stage, with a glimpse of the musicians who were sketched in the small and larger notebooks (**50**, Figs. 86, 87). Further sketches, sometimes redrawn in ink wash, showing singers, the conductor and views of the audience, bare-headed or top-hatted,[97] demonstrate the extent of Manet's interest in these café-concert scenes. One of the pencil sketches was evidently redrawn as an ink wash vignette, used to illustrate the catalogue of Manet's show in the gallery of *La Vie Moderne* in 1880 as well as an article by Goetschy in the magazine.[98] The fusion of motifs observed at an outdoor café-concert with his interior café scenes, suggests the degree of Manet's dependence on – and independence from – his 'real life' models.

Singers on stage – The final stage of the café-concert pictures *

It is quite possible that the concert motifs were added and final modifications to the café-concert pictures made almost at the same time, not long before the presentation of the London and Baltimore pictures in the exhibition at *La Vie Moderne*, in

88. **51**. Café singer and musicians. c.1878–80. Pencil on a double page from a notebook of smooth laid paper. 18.5 by 29.4 cm. (Musée du Louvre, Cabinet des Dessins, Paris.)

89. *Scene at a café-concert*. c.1878–80. Pencil on a double page from a notebook of smooth laid paper. 16.4 by 23.5 cm. (trimmed). (Musée du Louvre, Cabinet des Dessins, Paris.)

*See pp. 84–85.

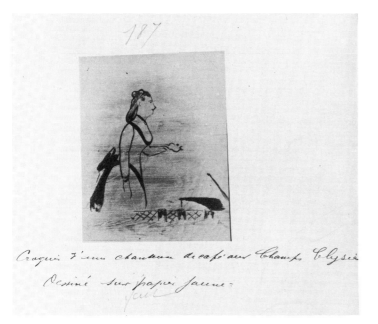

*Croquis d'une chanteuse de café aux Champs-Elysées
Dessiné sur papier jaune*

*Croquis dessiné sur papier jaune
Chanteuse de café-concert aux champs Elysées.*

90 and 91. *Chanteuse de café-concert aux Champs-Elysées (profil droite)* and *(profil gauche)*. c.1878–80. Photographs by Lochard, Nos.187 and 188, mounted on card and annotated (details). (Bernheim-Jeune archives, Paris.)

92. **52**. *La belle Polonaise*. c.1879–80. Transfer lithograph. 28.5 by 26.5 cm. (Bibliothèque Nationale, Cabinet des Estampes, Paris.)

April 1880. Indeed, one wonders whether the projected exhibition, in the galleries of a magazine devoted to the pastimes and pleasures of fashionable Parisians, may not have prompted the final transformation of Manet's canvases. His café scenes had a distinctly plebeian flavour, with their beer drinkers and unadorned settings. The notion of the café-concert immediately introduces a note of glamour, the sparkle of the footlights and the possibility of tropical references to a popular entertainer.

The London picture (**46**, Fig.82, Col. ill.5) has the most elaborate 'concert' scene, running right across the background. It shows a dancer on stage, caught in the glare of the gas footlights behind the high ramp, with the prompter's box on the left and a glimpse of the conductor's baton and sheet music; and in front of the stage, the musicians are exactly transcribed from Manet's drawings (**50** and **51**, Figs.86–88) and brushed in with a brilliance and freedom that evoke the pounding pace of the music. Manet had to fit them in between the foreground figures, and eliminated the waitress's right shoulder in order to accommodate the player with some kind of brass trumpet.

It was in making this final transformation of his original *Reichshoffen* composition that Manet finally resolved the formal and psychological balance of the London picture. The seated figures now all look towards the stage[99] and are perfectly counterbalanced by the waitress whose head Manet has turned, so that she ceases to draw the viewer into the picture space but brings the eye back to the world outside the picture frame. She now relates simultaneously to both background and foreground, and gives a sense of vitality and dynamism to the composition that is underlined by Manet's final, vivid brushstrokes on her face and dress, and the final placing of the beer mugs as a splash of brilliant colour against her blue-black dress.

The Paris canvas (**49**, Fig.85, Col. ill.7) already had a flatter, more ambiguous kind of picture space than the London picture. In the final addition of the café-concert motif, the stage setting is not actually shown, and there is an unexplained transition from a patterned wall or screen behind the waitress to the two-toned reddish ground that changes colour and perhaps plane behind the cropped and doll-like figure of the singer. Here, Manet apparently did not feel the need to turn away his waitress's head, although the softer, smiling features visible in the X-ray image (**48**, Fig.84) were firmed up, and Manet gave her a bolder, brassier stare.

The Baltimore picture (**54**, Fig.94, Col. ill.6), on which Manet apparently began work at the same time as the London fragment and its Paris variant (see the technical summary, p.85), was conceived from the start as a more dislocated group of figures. Although Manet wrestled his way through many adjustments of the background, the unchanged pose of the man in the top hat, gazing at something off towards the right, was from the start almost identical with the final pose adopted by the waitress in the London picture. The girl in the foreground may once have looked directly at the viewer, like Ellen Andrée in the Winterthur picture (**45**, Fig.81, Col. ill.4), but her final, unfocused stare and the set of her head relate to the overlapping background forms as well as to the objects on the table and the man beside her, so that the whole picture, including the mirrored reflection of the singer on a stage outside the picture space, is tied into a single plane.

The figures may appear to lack direct contact with each other – and have been interpreted as evidence of the alienation of the individual in urban society – but they are bound together, by purely pictorial means, into a close-knit social fabric. Mallarmé, in a characteristically dense passage, evoked Manet's total commitment to transcribing 'afresh, each time, being one with all, undifferentiated, deliberately', the 'fresh immediacy of the encounter'.[100]

Dates and exhibition dates – The café-concert pictures at La Vie Moderne

The left-hand, Winterthur section of Manet's *Reichshoffen* composition is clearly signed and dated 1878. The date on the London picture is unclear. It can be read as

93

94

93. **53.** *Café-concert.* Positive print from a
    composite X-radiograph of No. **54** (Fig. 94).
94. **54.** *Café-concert.* c.1878–80. 47.5 by
    39.2 cm. (The Walters Art Gallery,
    Baltimore.) Col. ill. 6.
95. **55.** *'La servante de bocks' (Café-concert).*
    1880. Brush and ink with gouache. 25.5 by
    21.5 cm. (The Burrell Collection, Glasgow.)

95

1878 or 1879, but since it now lies in the extreme lower left corner of the canvas, it was probably added to the original *Reichshoffen* composition when Manet was intending to send it to the Salon in 1878, before any of the subsequent modifications were made.[101] The inscription, in thin, fluid white paint, lies on a part of the canvas that was never subsequently reworked. The transformation of the London picture began after Barroil had returned the canvas to Manet at an unspecified date in 1879. In April 1880 the London and Baltimore pictures were listed as numbers 2 and 3, *Coin de café-concert* and *Café-concert*, in the catalogue of the exhibition of Manet's work shown at *La Vie Moderne*, so the café-concert pictures were completed by that date.

Manet made a drawing of the Baltimore *Café-concert* (**54**, Fig.94, Col.ill.6), which was reproduced in *La Vie Moderne* while his exhibition was on view.[102] The drawing (**55**, Fig.95), in brush and grey wash with corrections in white gouache (for the single tone, line-block reproduction), offers a lively, black-and-white interpretation of the painting, and was reproduced full-size in the magazine.[103]

All three café compositions were thus complete by the spring of 1880. In May the Salon opened, with Manet's *Chez le Père Lathuille*.[104] This painting shows a couple at a table, absorbed in their own relationship with each other while a waiter in the garden looks outwards, towards the viewer (Fig.13). It is, in a sense, a reworking – though with striking modifications – of the 'conversation piece' that Manet had attempted in his original *Reichshoffen* composition. In the final transformation of his cafés into café-concert scenes, Manet was able to break his last ties with the world of the closed composition and a traditional use of perspective (with all the problems of scale and spatial relationships that that had always implied for an artist who wished to paint with an innocent eye, and without reference to established 'rules').

The final version of the London picture (**46**, Fig.82, Col.ill.5), with its last-minute resolution, and the brilliant invention of the mirror motif in the Baltimore picture (**54**, Fig.94, Col.ill.6), led on to Manet's last great project in which he distilled the accumulated experience of his whole career. He still had to wrestle, like Jacob with the angel, to achieve his final result, and the preparatory oil sketch as well as the visible or 'hidden' transformations in *A bar at the Folies-Bergère* (**59–62**, Figs.101–104, Col.ills.8, 9) are a demonstration of the artist's creative processes which remained essentially unchanged from the days of the *Nymphe surprise* and *Déjeuner sur l'herbe* (see pp.26–42), but were now operating on a quite different level of maturity.

A Bar at the Folies-Bergère

By 1879, Manet was seriously beginning to feel the effects of his syphilis. He began to follow treatments of various kinds and spent some time in September and October 1879 at a hydrotherapy establishment at Bellevue, on the outskirts of Paris. It was there that he met Émilie Ambre, who persuaded him to allow her to take the great painting of the *Execution of Maximilian* (**37**, Fig.71, Col.ill.11) to America (see pp.61–62). In 1880 she rented him a house where he spent most of the summer following his treatment, and in 1881 he spent the whole summer at Versailles, under another doctor.

According to Léon Leenhoff, it was during that summer of 1881 that Manet painted the composition sketch of *A bar at the Folies-Bergère* (**60**, Fig.102, Col. ill.8).[105] The subject of Manet's final Salon painting was a major undertaking and once again the composition was based on drawings and pastels (Figs.97, 98), made in preparation for the picture which was developed in several complex stages until it reached its final form.

As with the drawings made at a café-concert on the Champs-Elysées (Figs.90, 91), annotations and descriptions in Léon's register and on the Lochard photograph cards identify the works made directly or indirectly from scenes observed at the Folies-Bergère. Manet's painting was of course a studio work, but he distilled into it very specific notations. A study of his drawings and sketches, together with the X-radiograph evidence of the oil sketch and final painting, as well as reference to contemporary documents, demonstrates the fine balance of observed reality and pictorial fiction which gives this picture its magical and disturbing qualities.

The place

This most Parisian of all variety theatres was opened in 1869 on the rue Richer. It played an important role in the life of the capital, and even served, in February 1871, as an electoral meeting place for the presentation of candidates for the National Assembly.[106] In 1878, an article was published, describing the delights of the newly embellished establishment. The text gives a very clear idea of the atmosphere Manet was recreating in his painting, and is worth quoting extensively.

> What is the first thing the foreigner asks for when he reaches Paris? The Folies-Bergère.
>
> Because there more than anywhere else you find the very essence of the city. You can see the Parisian way of life there, as though unveiled; you can join in the life of this whole world, in all its lightness, aimiability, panache, charm, polish, dazzling brilliance and sophisticated mockery, whose tastes [the director] has so successfully understood. . . . The soul of Paris is concentrated and inhaled in this soft, perfumed atmosphere. . . .
>
> There are bars everywhere . . . tended by charming girls whose playful glances and delightful smiles attract a swarm of customers.
>
> [The director] has filled his magic garden with every seduction. The Hanlon-Lees team, pantomimes, ballets, music that carries one away . . . nothing has been left out of this wide range of pleasures.
>
> The eye is enchanted, the ear charmed, and you are captivated, dazzled by it all.[107]

Manet and the theatre

The masterpiece in which Manet celebrated his own delight in the world of the Folies-Bergère grew from the observed realities of his own experience. In the spring of 1877, the *Revue de la Semaine* published a print from an ink wash drawing by Manet (**56**, Fig. 96). Entitled *Au Paradis*, 'In the gods', it shows spectators in the upper balcony of a variety theatre, looking down towards the action out of sight on the stage. The scene is very close to that in a drawing identified on the Lochard photograph card as a 'Pen drawing executed from sketches made at the Folies-Bergère' (Fig. 97),[108] which was probably made with a similar print in mind.

In Léon's register, the composition sketch for the *Bar* (**60**, Fig. 102, Col. ill. 8) is described under No. 265: 'Sketch for the Bar at the Folies-Bergère. First idea for the picture. It is the bar on the first floor, to the right of the stage and the proscenium. Portrait of Dupray. Was painted in the summer of 1881.'[109] The information on the Lochard photograph card is more detailed: 'Painted from sketches made at the Folies-Bergère. Henri Dupray is talking to the barmaid in the studio on the rue d'Amsterdam.'[110] Henri Dupray was a painter of military subjects who had a studio at 70 rue d'Amsterdam, in the same building as Rosen, whose studio Manet occupied temporarily in 1878–79.

Léon's precise identification of the view shown in the *Bar* can be checked against a seating plan of the theatre of 1875 (**57**, Fig. 99). The 'bar on the first floor to the right of the stage and proscenium' (presumably as one looks at the stage), would have been placed against the wall of the first floor gallery, between two of the flat pilasters with large gas globes which are seen, reflected from across the theatre, in the great mirror on the wall behind the barmaid. This mirror, in both

REVUE DE LA SEMAINE.

AU PARADIS.

Dessin inédit de MANET.

96. **56.** *Au paradis.* (In the gods.) 1877. Transfer
lithograph. 20.5 by 25.7 cm. (subject),
29 by 43.7 cm. (printed letters). Published
in the *Revue de la Semaine* [April 1877].
(The British Museum, London.)

97. *Aux Folies-Bergère.* c.1878–80. Photograph
by Lochard, No.247, mounted on card and
annotated (detail). 1883. (Bernheim-Jeune
archives, Paris.)

sketch and final painting, clearly shows the huge chandeliers which appear in the
plan (**57**, Fig.99) and also in an engraving made a few years earlier (**58**, Fig.100).

The seating plan announces 'A variety of spectacles – Operettas – Ballets –
English pantomimes – Acrobats – Gymnasts – Eccentricities of every kind', and
one of the most popular turns, from the early 1870s, was the American acrobatic
troupe known as the Hanlon-Lees brothers and Little Bob, whose poster had
appeared on the window in the Winterthur half of Manet's *Reichshoffen* composition
(**45**, Fig.81, Col.ill.4) three years earlier. In an engraving of 1872, they are shown
flying through the air above a safety net in the main body of the theatre (**58**,
Fig.100). This illustration explains one of the wittiest elements in Manet's *Bar*: the
legs ending in bright green bootees that appear on a trapeze in the upper left
corner of the large painting. If the bar was set up against the side wall of the
theatre, the position of the figure on the trapeze relates perfectly to an act such as
that of the Hanlon-Lees, or the 'Représentations de Miss Leona Dare', who per-
formed stupefying stunts on a trapeze at the Folies-Bergère in 1876.[111]

Besides coinciding with plans and engraved views of the Folies-Bergère, Manet's
composition also relates closely to one of the drawings documented as being 'from
sketches made at the Folies-Bergère' (Fig.97).[112] Like the *Au Paradis* print (**56**, Fig.96),
it shows figures in the balcony, seen from below as they peer down towards the
stage. The row of heads passes in front of what looks like a flat pilaster and the
effect of the swiftly-handled brush drawing is close to that of the shorthand
dashes and blobs of paint that describe a very similar view in the upper left corner
of the sketch for the *Bar* (**60**, Fig.102, Col.ill.8).

98. *Portrait de Méry Laurent, pastel fait d'après
une photographie.* 1881. Photograph by
Lochard, No.138, mounted on card and
annotated (detail). c.1883. (Bernheim-Jeune
archives, Paris.)

The Amsterdam sketch *

The composition sketch for the *Bar* (**60**, Fig.102, Col.ill.8) was recently examined
and X-radiographed.[113] The canvas was found to have been cut on three sides – at
the top, bottom and left edges – and restretched. The present format is now more
square than that of the large Courtauld painting (**62**, Fig.104, Col.ill.9), and it is
not easy to assess the original format and design of the composition sketch.

*See pp.85–86.

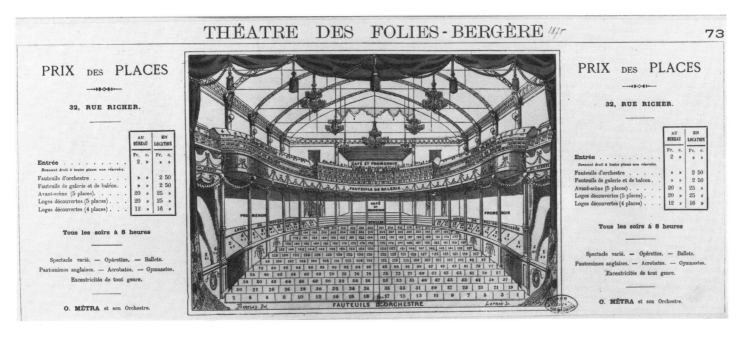

99. **57.** *Théâtre des Folies-Bergère*, by Barclay. 1875. Seating plan, printed by Lefman and hand-coloured. 15.5 by 38.5 cm. (Bibliothèque Nationale, Cabinet des Estampes, Paris.)

Against the reflection in the mirror, with its lively crowds of spectators and shimmering chandeliers, the barmaid stands off-centre to the right,[114] with hands clasped, leaning forward across her almost empty counter to look down at the little man beyond the limits of the picture space but seen in reflection, to the right. The figures are startlingly different from those in the large painting, but X-ray evidence has shown that they were in fact Manet's point of departure.

The Courtauld picture *

How did Manet move from the loosely constructed, very different design of the Amsterdam sketch to the strange and monumental composition of the Courtauld painting (**62**, Fig.104, Col.ill.9)? The evidence recently supplied by X-radiography of the Courtauld picture (**61**, Fig.103),[115] shows that Manet transferred his sketch design to the large canvas and made all further alterations in the course of work. Beneath the present surface of the Courtauld picture, with the barmaid's displaced reflection and the head of the man she faces represented in the upper right corner of the canvas, lies the whole composition seen in the sketch (**60**, Fig.102, Col.ill.8).

If the barmaid in the Amsterdam and Courtauld pictures is compared, in terms of her relative size and position within the two compositions, she is seen, in the Courtauld picture, to be centrally placed and greatly enlarged and monumentalised: here, her head is almost at the top of the picture, while her arms, originally crossed as in the sketch and now extended to support her as she leans on the bar, emphasise the greater length of the figure visible above the marble surface.

As to her celebrated reflection, and its encounter with the top-hatted gentleman in the upper corner, Manet did not reach his final solution at one bound. The X-ray image shows, in between the first reflection in the mirror, echoing that of the sketch, and its final position at the right edge, the whole shape of the girl's back, with her profile, white collar and shoulder echoing the outlines of these same shapes in their first and final positions. The X-radiograph also solves another mystery in the final, surface design: it shows that as laid-in, in its final position on the right, the reflection of the barmaid was somewhat different, her waist and hips were much slimmer, and she was leaning forward, with her arms still bent at the elbow, just like the 'real' girl in the sketch. The decision to straighten the barmaid's arms and give her a more upright pose in the Courtauld picture was therefore made at a late stage in the development of the composition.

All the alterations visible in the X-ray image prompt one to wonder whether the barmaid's head and face in the Courtauld picture were once closer to their appear-

100. **58.** *Folies-Bergère. Représentations des Frères Hanlon-Lees et de Little Bob, Gymnastes Americains*, by Beaurepaire after Truchon. November 1872. Wood-engraving. 33.5 by 23.5 cm. (Bibliothèque Nationale, Cabinet des Estampes, Paris.)

*See p.86.

101

101. **59**. Sketch for *Un bar aux Folies-Bergère*.
Positive print from a composite
X-radiograph of No. **60** (Fig. 102).

102. **60**. Sketch for *Un bar aux Folies-Bergère*.
1881. 47 by 56 cm. (Stedelijk Museum,
Amsterdam. On loan from
Dr. F. F. R. Koenigs.) Col. ill. 8.

103. **61**. *Un bar aux Folies-Bergère*. Positive
print from a composite X-radiograph of
No. **62** (Fig. 104).

104. **62**. *Un bar aux Folies-Bergère*. Signed and
dated 1882. 96 by 130 cm. (Courtauld
Institute Galleries, London.) Col. ill. 9.

103

102

104

ance in the sketch. But the face is freshly painted, with the canvas priming showing through, as it does in the pendant at her neck and the flowers at her breast. The only other areas of the Courtauld picture that remain thinly covered are the front of the balcony and the figure of Méry Laurent leaning on it, with her long yellow gloves. This 'portrait', noted in Léon Leenhoff's description of the canvas, was painted from a 'pastel made from a photograph', according to another of his annotations in the register and on the Lochard photograph cards (Fig. 98).[116]

The rest of the painting is either extensively reworked or is thickly painted over the laying-in layer. This is clearly the case with the still-life of bottles, flower vase and fruit on the table – a still-life composed in Manet's studio and bearing no relationship to what the real bar must have looked like, as more realistically suggested in the Amsterdam sketch. The still-life is one of Manet's triumphs in the genre, the fruit and flower and bottles painted with as much relish as his succulent ham of a few years earlier (II, Fig. 19), and it gives a revealing glimpse of Manet's preferences, with the bottles of Bass pale ale (identifiable by the familiar red triangle on the labels) beside the champagne bottles improbably warming-up on the counter.[117] Even the inclusion of the glass bowl of mandarins was a piece of sheer self-indulgence, and recalls Manet's expressions of delight after the sale of his cafe painting (**45**, Fig. 81, Col. ill. 4) to M. Barroil. Manet described him as a 'gentleman' because he sent the artist from Marseille 'a case of mandarins, a bit of his sunshine', which Manet then distributed to the street urchins, commenting that they would probably prefer money but that he was giving them what gave him pleasure.[118]

Georges Jeanniot, a young military officer who was also a painter, paid a visit to Manet in January 1882. He found him at work on the *Bar*, and has left a fascinating account of the artist in his studio: 'He was painting the *Bar at the Folies-Bergère*, and the model, a pretty girl, was posing behind a table laden with bottles and food. . . . I took a seat behind him and watched him work. Although he worked from the model, Manet didn't copy nature at all closely; I noted his bold simplifications. . . . Everything was simplified: the tones were made lighter, the colours brighter, the values were more closely related to each other, the tones made more contrasting. It all resolved itself into a soft, blonde harmony.' Jeanniot returned on other occasions and reported Manet's advice to him, cited in John House's essay (see p. 17), ending with a final admonition to avoid falling into the everyday banality that comes from paying too much attention to the information provided by the natural world: 'You must always keep the upper hand and do something amusing. Nothing laboured! oh no, nothing laboured! . . .'[119]

From the moment he sketched in the trapeze and the acrobat's legs – just visible in the upper left corner of the Amsterdam sketch (**60**, Fig. 102, Col. ill. 8) – painted the piled-up blonde hair and pert features of the barmaid and staged her relationship to Henri Dupray, who eyes her quizzically, holding his gold-knobbed cane to his chin, Manet gave free rein to his wit and invention. The large *Bar* (**62**, Fig. 104, Col. ill. 9) is a tapestry woven from fragments of reality, masterfully composed, subtly blended and magnificently painted. From the sketches in his notebooks (Fig. 97), from the dots, squiggles and *taches* (as summary and as lively as those in his *Music in the Tuileries*[120] of twenty years earlier) in the Amsterdam sketch (**60**, Fig. 102, Col. ill. 8), Manet built up his Salon picture with the combination of skill, flair and intuition that Mallarmé understood so well.

There is not one dull passage in the painting. Every area is full of interest and observation, even the hazy, mirrored view of the columns and crowd of theatre-goers beneath the balcony. And under the mirrored chandeliers and suggestion of the great circular sweep of the theatre interior, Manet has depicted '*le tout Paris*', with pocket portraits of celebrated beauties that were no doubt instantly recognisable to the friends who frequented this world. Some of them we know. Méry Laurent, the demi-mondaine, adored by Mallarmé and Manet, is a 'star' in her white dress and long yellow gloves.[121] Immediately behind her, in a box, is the fashionable young actress, Jeanne Demarsy.[122] And although no means of identifying them survives, the woman looking through her opera glasses and another with a fan were no doubt also based on sketches and studies of particular people.

On a very grand scale, with the mirror motif taking over the whole of the background, Manet restates in the *Bar at the Folies-Bergère*, many of the basic ideas in the Baltimore *Café-concert* (**54**, Fig.94, Col. ill.6). But with the final, iconic pose and inscrutable gaze of his blonde barmaid, he comes full circle, to the frontal confrontation with the viewer that makes *Olympia* (**30**, Fig.56), painted some twenty years earlier, such a disturbing figure. Both figures, the professional model as prostitute and the real-life barmaid re-enacting her rôle in the artist's studio, are lifted far beyond the confines of their original, anecdotal context and made into richly symbolic images.

Conclusion

In the early sixties with the *Déjeuner sur l'herbe* and *Olympia*, in the late sixties with the *Execution of Maximilian*, in the late seventies with his 'Reichshoffen' composition and the café-concert series and, finally, in the *Bar at the Folies-Bergère*, Manet explores and adjusts the relationship of figure to figure and figure to setting. In these works he is constantly searching for perfect formal balance, the most telling relationship with the viewer and the fullest expression of his idea.

As one stands, like Jeanniot, almost watching Manet paint his pictures (probing the evidence of their actual surface, using scientific aids like X-rays, and sifting the clues in sketches, prints and drawings), the pictures themselves reveal his knowledge and love of his *métier*, the freedom and wit of his inventions, the dogged commitment that led him, sometimes with such difficulty, to the final form of his great masterpieces. Manet began as a student of Titian, impudently clothing high renaissance forms in modern dress. Twenty years later, and already in the shadow of death, his images of modernity had found the classic balance and the sublime artifice of a great Titian *poesia*.

Technical summary

The café pictures

At this stage of research into the physical development of the *Reichshoffen* composition and the two paintings directly derived from it, as well as the conception and evolution of the Paris and Baltimore pictures (and in the absence of an X-radiograph of the Winterthur picture), one can only list, and attempt to plot chronologically, the known changes in the various compositions:

Reichshoffen   Original design – Reconstruction (**42**, Fig. 77)
The canvas was cropped at top and bottom by the time the differing formats of the Winterthur and London fragments had been established; the table had already been extended towards, if not to meet, the lower edge of the canvas (the line marking the extension is clearly visible behind the match holder, and runs across the table in both the Winterthur and London pictures); this extension covered the side of the chair on which Ellen Andrée rests her hand, and which was at one time in front of the table, whose left edge was also slightly extended.

The Winterthur canvas (**45**, Fig. 81, Col. ill. 4)
Ellen Andrée's head is very freely and thinly painted, with the canvas priming showing through; Guérard, next to her, appears more thickly but still freshly painted; the head of the girl in profile is very thickly painted; her grey and black costume was thinly brushed over the still wet, dark brownish surface below the window, and has cracked extensively; the girl's hands were added before the final cutting of the canvas, since her fingertips and part of her napkin are found on the London painting.

The London canvas (**46** and **47**, Figs. 82, 83, Col. ill. 5)
Beneath the background, now totally repainted with the café-concert motifs, the X-ray image (**47**, Fig. 83) shows the continuation of the *Reichshoffen* window seen in the Winterthur canvas (and corresponding to its position in the drawing, **43**, Fig. 79); the right side of the waitress's head was originally placed where Manet cut the canvas, at (2); comparison with the Paris picture and its X-ray image (**48** and **49**, Figs. 84, 85) suggests that she originally faced the viewer; she was apparently repainted in her new position, with her head above that of the seated man, before the addition of a wide strip of canvas to the right; her arm and skirt and the man's blue smock were then extended over the new piece of canvas; the London X-radiograph shows that she held the beer mugs lower, as in the Paris picture; the outline of the man's left elbow was corrected and the position of his hand and pipe was raised, obscuring the profile of the man in the grey hat.

In the final alterations, a background showing a stage, performer and musicians was added, extending over the full width of the original canvas and the additional strip; the waitress's sleeve at her elbow was brought within the limit of the picture, probably when the beer mugs were raised; her right shoulder was suppressed to make room for one of the musicians; and final adjustments were made to her head and collar; the turning of her head, to look away to the right, necessitated the alteration of its shape – seen in the X-ray and on the paint surface – and the painting out of the curls on her forehead.

The Paris canvas (**48** and **49**, Figs.84, 85, Col. ill.7)
The X-ray image shows the light window area at the left edge, suggesting that the painting was originally based on part of Manet's *Reichshoffen* design; the paint layer that extends around the left side of the stretcher is as thin towards the top (extending from beneath the café singer to the cut edge of the canvas) as on the picture surface lower down; it shows the light colours found in the Winterthur window (and in the paint samples taken from this area in the London canvas), and a light green area that could be related to the poster; around the side of the stretcher at lower left, there appear to be traces of the wine glass that stands in front of the beer mug in the London picture.

On the upper surface and around the top edge of the stretcher is an underlying paint layer of deep reddish brown (showing a mixture of dark red and vermilion); over this layer was added a floral pattern of red flowers on green leaves, and over this again the yellow stripes with a dragged grey overlay, the broad green edging band, the gas lamps and the two tones of red and orange behind the singer, who is added as a 'cut-out' figure, exactly split down the centre, on the new canvas edge; her dress overlaps the hat of the young woman.

Around the lower edge of the stretcher, the man's blue smock continues without a break to the limit of the cut canvas. The X-radiograph shows the waitress's face to have been softer and her expression smiling; her left shoulder extended to the right edge of the canvas, and was later touched out and brought within the picture when the stripes were added on the wallpaper.

The Baltimore canvas (**53** and **54**, Figs.93, 94, Col. ill.6)
Like the London and Paris pictures, this is also a cut canvas, trimmed on the left and upper edges. Gifford [1984/85] has given a very clear account of its evolution, with almost every aspect of the canvas changing except for the top-hatted gentleman and the cut-off figure on the right. Like the other pictures, it originally had a deep red background colour, and then the same floral pattern and the same green and yellow stripes with dragged grey as the Paris picture; this was followed by a patterned blue layer, before the final blue-grey background with the mirror on the left.

The figure at lower left was originally dressed in black, and then blue, with a hat painted directly over the floral wallpaper, before the final beige dress that recalls Ellen Andrée's coat in the Winterthur picture.

The X-radiograph is confused as a result of all the scraping and repainting, but clearly shows the changes in the foreground, including the beer mug removed from under Edmond André's hand and placed at the right edge of the canvas, and the resulting shift of the wine glass with a spoon from right to far right, leaving a double image on the X-radiograph.

A bar at the Folies-Bergère

The Amsterdam sketch (**59** and **60**, Figs.101, 102, Col. ill.8)
Compared with the Courtauld picture (**62**, Fig.104, Col. ill.9), the scene on the surface of the sketch extends farther to the left and top: it rises well above the head of the barmaid, showing much more of the chandeliers (and the central one, immediately above the barmaid's head, extends around the top edge of the stretcher, to the cut edge of the canvas); at the left edge, there is more space to the left of the reflected pilaster, with just an indication of the trapeze and legs at upper left, and the edge of the black-fronted bar is visible. The whole of the painted area on the left continues round the side of the stretcher to the cut edge of the canvas, and with it the original left side of the bar. On the reduced surface of the canvas, the end of the bar is indicated with pinkish paint over the black in the lower left corner; at this stage also, the light, top surface of the bar was painted in, ending just before the new left edge of the restretched canvas.

At the top of the picture, a pinkish-red horizontal band of paint runs right across the upper edge of the canvas, and extends around the left and upper edges of the stretcher to the limits of the cut canvas. Since the uppermost, central chandelier above the barmaid's head is painted over this band, it probably represents an architectural feature (although its position as a reflected element, in relation to the chandeliers, is unclear).

The blonde barmaid wears a dress that was originally high-necked and bright Prussian blue. She was then given a wide and deep *décolleté*, with a flesh tone brushed hastily over the blue dress (and her bare forearms may have been added at this stage, since the canvas priming only shows around her hands). Elsewhere her dress was transformed by overpainting in grey-black tones. The outline of her piled-up blonde hair, tied with a light blue ribbon, has been corrected in pencil, with a corresponding line on the hair in her reflection. The X-ray image (**59**, Fig.101) confirms that the picture was painted with great freshness and spontaneity and was hardly altered in the course of work. The one change that occurred – visible both in the X-ray and on the canvas surface – was the moving of the little man even further down and to the right.

The Courtauld picture (**61** and **62**, Figs.103, 104, Col.ill.9)
The Courtauld X-ray image (**61**, Fig.103) shows that the theatre balcony was originally as deep as in the sketch: its darker area shows to a line level with the girl's hips, as in the sketch, and corresponding, in the final picture, to a line about halfway down the reflected image of the table, just below the tops of the champagne bottles in the foreground. The reflected table itself extended farther to the left, its side edge running back behind the beer bottle, rather than the champagne bottles.

Although the barmaid stands, apparently from the moment the large picture was laid-in, in a central position, her arms were crossed loosely in front of her, as in the sketch, her reflection appeared in the same 'normal' position, just to the right (a curved outline on the X-radiograph, just above the fruit bowl, represents the highlight on her shoulder, and the shape of her reflected head is just visible over the pilaster behind), and the little man, with his bowler hat, white collar and stick, appeared at the right edge of the composition (and is now completely hidden by the final position of the girl's reflection).

In straightening the girl's arms, Manet broadened the whole outline of the figure. Her right arm now completely hides a champagne bottle that is clearly visible in the X-ray image. Once again, this explains an anomaly in the final picture: with the arm in place, Manet extended the shape of the neighbouring beer bottle, so that where it had stood *behind* the champagne bottles which mirror those on the foreground table top, it now appears in front of them, making nonsense of the mirror view.

Notes

1 See WILSON BAREAU [1984], p.757, App.I, No.3.

2 See the exh. cat. Paris/New York [1983], No.19.

3 See notes 7 and 19.

4 Examples of the subject are found in paintings by Veronese and Romanelli, both from the royal collections and both engraved for the album, or *recueil*, published by the eighteenth-century financier and connoisseur, Pierre Crozat, which Manet could have seen in the Cabinet des Estampes at the Bibliothèque impériale. Veronese: Envoi d'Etat à Dijon in 1812; engraved by Edmé Jeaurat. Romanelli, Inv.575, Musée de Compiègne by 1850; engraved by Simon Vallée.

5 Knut Berg, Director of the Nasjonalgalleriet in Oslo, was kind enough to authorise this, and Leif Einar Plahter, chief restorer, gave expert and enthusiastic help in interpreting the results.

6 In his drawings, still unclassified according to paper types and therefore difficult to study in sequence and to date, copies of works in Roman collections and of those in Florentine churches and museums are apparently drawn on the same sketchbook pages.

7 'Manet avait commencé rue Lavoisier un grand tableau, "Moïse sauvé des eaux", qu'il n'a jamais achevé. . . .' Proust [1897], p.168. For Manet's various apartments and studios, see the exh. cat. Paris/New York [1983], pp.502–18.

8 The fact that the drawing is made up of one page and several fragments from one of Manet's early 'Italian' notebooks, suggests that the pencil underdrawing of the main part of the design – the figure of the woman – may be directly derived from an Italian source. Jennifer Montagu has pointed out to me the similarity with one of the figures in Raphael's *Fire in the Borgo* fresco in the Vatican in Rome, from which Manet made a superb red chalk drawing in his large 'Italian' album (Louvre, Dessins, RF 30.431, RW II, 37). A detail from Raphael's *School of Athens* also appears in two different 'Italian' notebooks (Louvre, RF 30.460, RW II, 33; Louvre, RF 30.434, Leiris 237).

9 M. CURTISS: 'Letters of Edouard Manet to his Wife during the Siege of Paris 1870–71', *Apollo* [June 1981], pp.378–79.

10 See F. HARTT: *Giulio Romano*, New Haven [1958], II, No.335.

11 This was the *Histoire de Bethsabée*, frontispiece and three plates by J. Corneille le Jeune (1646–1695): (DUMESNIL, VI [1842], p.323). Several complete sets, as well as single plates, are in the Cabinet des Estampes, including one from the Devéria collection (see the B.N. *Inventaire*). The first subject shows Bathsheba at the bath, the second Bathsheba at her toilet.

12 See note 8 above.

13 See the exh. cat. Paris/New York [1983], No.12.

14 See FARWELL [1975], pp.224–29; REFF [1970], pp.456–58.

15 See the exh. cat. Paris/New York [1983], No.33.

16 The recent reappearance of the portrait of Ambroise Adam (see *op. cit.* in note 1 above), supports the idea that there was probably a painting behind every early etching by Manet.

17 A first, rough grouping of Manet's drawings by format and type of paper, has produced a count of over twenty different 'albums' or 'sketchbooks', two or three of them virtually intact, but the majority represented by only a few sheets.

18 The drawing in the Boymans-van Beuningen Museum, Rotterdam (**8**, Fig.33), hitherto only ascribed to Manet, is on the same type of paper, has the same light underdrawing in red chalk, and exactly the same handling of the wash with a broad pen and brush as the celebrated drawing recorded in Manet's studio and acquired by Degas at the 1884 sale (**9**, Fig.34). The less expert handling of the wash technique in the Rotterdam drawing no doubt explains the *reprise* in a second version. Absent from the *œuvre* catalogues of Manet's drawings, it is described in the catalogue of the Boymans Museum, *Franse Tekeningen uit de 19e Eeuw*, ed. H. R. HOETINK, Rotterdam [1968], No.187.

19 'De 1858 à 1860, il fait une série d'études, "l'Etudiant de Salamanque", "Moïse sauvé des eaux", "la Toilette", "la Promenade" . . .' PROUST [1901], p.72. The subject of the first of these *études* was an allegory based on Le Sage's preface to *Gil Blas*, signed and dated by Manet in 1860 (RW 28); see MAUNER [1975], pp.164–65. *The promenade* can probably be identified with another 'allegory', the costume piece already referred to (Fig.29 and

note 13), in which Manet and Suzanne appear as Rubens and Hélène Fourment, walking in the countryside near the Seine, on the Ile Saint-Ouen (in the suburbs to the north of Paris, where the Manet family owned property). This was apparently also the setting for *The Salamanca students*.

20 See notes 13 and 19. For the Crozat *recueil*, see note 26.

21 These were first pointed out by FARWELL [1975], p.229.

22 The date is attested by the Dépôt légal by Godet of twenty-four photographs of paintings by Manet on 3rd April 1872, under the numbers 851–874 (B. N. Estampes, *Etats des Depots de la Librairie* [1872–73]). Fifteen of the works had been acquired by Durand-Ruel as part of his massive purchase from Manet's studio in January of the same year. See the exh. cat. Paris/New York [1983], No.118, Provenance.

23 Lochard's photographs of the works in Manet's studio were numbered in accordance with the works in Léon's register (see note 52 below, and the Bibliography).

24 Tintoretto, *Suzanne au bain*, Paris, Louvre (Inv.568). It is significant that at this early stage in his career, Manet felt bound to create a new meaning, a new *raison d'être* for his bather, once she had been torn from her original context in the large composition.

25 To Michel Laclotte, Inspecteur-Général des Musées chargé des Collections du Musée d'Orsay, who gave his authorisation, and to the Director and staff of the Laboratoire de Recherche des Musées de France, who carried out this work, are due the warmest thanks for their cooperation. In particular, Maurice Solier, chief radiographer at the Laboratoire, not only produced an X-radiograph of superb quality of this huge canvas, carefully calculated to bring out all the details of the setting (although this was inevitably of some detriment to the rendering of the nude), but also made perfect copies of this and other X-radiographs of Musée d'Orsay pictures for use in this publication and the exhibition.

26 Proust recorded that Manet had copied the *Concert champêtre* in the Louvre as a student, referring to the painting in the following terms: 'Quand nous étions à l'atelier, j'ai copié les femmes de Giorgione, les femmes avec les musiciens. Il est noir ce tableau. Les fonds ont repoussé. Je veux refaire cela et le faire dans la transparence de l'atmosphère, avec des personnages comme nous voyons là-bas.' (They were watching boats sailing and women bathing in the Seine at Argenteuil at the time.) PROUST [1897], p.171.

The engraving after the 'Giorgione' *Pastorale* was published in the *Recueil d'estampes d'après les plus beaux tableaux et d'après les plus beaux dessins qui sont en France*, Paris, Imprimerie royale [1729 and 1742], 3 vols. The work was edited by Pierre Crozat (1665–1740), the financier and collector who was Watteau's patron. (Cabinet des Estampes, Bibiothèque Nationale, Paris, Aa 57.)

27 See the preceding note.

28 Notebook of *c*.1861–62 (Pierpont Morgan Library, New York), RW II, 678 and 679. See the exh. cat. Paris/New York [1983], No.31.

29 TABARANT [1947], p.76.

30 The subject of the great Titian painting in the Louvre was identified until recently as *Jupiter and Antiope*, that is, the Ovidian story of the god in the form of a satyr unveiling a nymph.

31 Crozat owned a version of the Titian *Danaë* in the Prado Museum, Madrid, and it was engraved for his *recueil* (see note 26); it is now in the Hermitage, Leningrad. See note 33.

32 This could perhaps be an allusion to the gesture of the *Venus pudica*.

33 Manet's travels in Italy are uncertain, but if he went to Rome, as seems highly likely, he may have gone as far as Naples, where he could have seen Titian's earlier *Danaë* in the Capodimonte Gallery. An engraving after the Naples *Danaë* appeared in Charles Blanc's *Histoire des Peintres* and it is worth noting that in this version a fold of drapery lies over Danaë's right thigh (Fig.52a).

34 All the other works that are in any way related to the theme, the water-colour (RW II, 381), the etchings, and above all the drawings of an *Odalisque* and a *Woman with a cat* (RW II, 366 and 379), were made later, particularly the last two, which should almost certainly be dated in the late 1860s and early 1870s respectively.

35 The negress appears almost as a variant on the dark-skinned gypsy woman who holds up her apron to catch the shower of gold in some versions of Titian's *Danaë*, including the one shown here (27, Fig.53).

36 A. CLAIRET: 'Le Bracelet de l'Olympia – Genèse et Destinée d'un Chef-d'oeuvre', *L'Oeil*, No.333 [April 1983], p.37.

37 Baudelaire's much-quoted letter to Manet at the time of its exhibition could suggest that he had in fact seen the painting before he left Paris in 1864, but not its final form. See the exh. cat. Paris/New York [1983], No.64. The signature and date appear on the dark edge of the bed, a part of the painting that was not altered.

Furthermore, Manet's portrait of Zacharie Astruc (Kunsthalle, Bremen; RW 92; see the exh. cat. Paris/New York [1983], No.94) may also prove relevant to this discussion. Astruc, who composed the verse that was affixed to *Olympia*'s frame and printed in the 1865 Salon catalogue, sat for his portrait in Manet's studio. The portrait, apparently dated 1866, places Astruc in a setting that evokes both Titian's *Venus of Urbino* in the 'view' on the left (see 28, Fig.54) and Manet's own *Olympia* in the similarly edged wall or screen (or frame?) behind the sitter (Fig.56). Could Astruc be sitting beside a not-so-fanciful representation of the still incomplete *Olympia*?

38 Granted that there may have been a painted version of *La toilette* (14, Fig.39 – see note 19), this could be seen as a variation on the presentation of a nude in an interior, possibly executed between the earlier and later versions of the reclining figure.

39 Repainted fragment (Chicago Art Institute), RW 98; water-colour after the whole composition (Fogg Art Museum, Cambridge, Mass.), RW II, 548.

40 The John G. Johnson Collection, Philadelphia. RW 76; exh. cat. Paris/New York [1983], No.83. See note 44.

41 *Le fifre* (Orsay, Paris). RW 113; Paris/New York [1983], No.93. *L'acteur tragique* (National Gallery of Art, Washington, D.C.). RW 106; Paris/New York [1983], No.89.

42 See the account by MEREDITH J. STRANG: 'Napoleon III: The Fatal Foreign Policy', in the exh. cat. Brown University [1981], pp.83–99.

43 *L'Exposition universelle de 1867* (Nasjonalgalleriet, Oslo), RW 123.

44 In 1864, in the window of a well-known print shop, Manet had exhibited a picture recording a sensational event that had just occurred, when an episode in the American Civil War was played out off the Normandy coast: this was the sinking of a Confederate supply ship by a Union gunboat near Cherbourg. See the exh. cat. Paris/New York [1983], No.83.

45 See SANDBLAD [1954], the pioneering study; Brown University [1981], a comprehensive investigation; and the dossier in the exh. cat. Paris/New York [1983], Appendix II.

46 See M. WILSON [1983], p.28ff. We are very grateful to Michael Wilson for his cooperation in obtaining permission from the Ny Carlsberg Glyptotek to undertake this examination and for arranging for X-radiographs to be made at the National Gallery.

47 See FONSMARK [1984]. Anne-Birgitte Fonsmark, curator at the Ny Carlsberg Glyptotek, and Henrik Bjerre, chief restorer at the Statens Museum for Kunst, gave valuable assistance and were most helpful in examining the picture in Copenhagen.

48 Roland Dorn, curator at the Städtische Kunsthalle Mannheim, collaborated to the full in the initial examination of the painting, and the Director, Manfred Fath, was an enthusiastic supporter of the project to get the painting to Munich. He found the means to achieve this and once there, it was expertly examined, cleaned and restored by the Director of the Doerner Institute, Hubertus Falkner von Sonnenburg, who generously discussed the painting and communicated photographs and negatives for this publication and the exhibition.

David Bomford discussed the existing X-radiographs at The National Gallery, London. Peter Sutton, Baker Curator of European Paintings, at the Boston Museum of Fine Arts, arranged for the X-radiography of the Boston canvas almost as this text was going to press.

49 See the exh. cat. Brown University [1981], pp.116–17. All contemporary accounts referred to here are quoted or translated from the original French texts transcribed and compiled by PAMELA M. JONES: 'Appendix: Documentation', *op. cit.*, pp.116–22.

50 See Manet's letter to Fantin, cit. MOREAU-NELATON [1926], I, p.72.

51 See the exh. cat. Paris/New York [1983], No.104.

52 There is a confusion, which has never been pointed out or explained, between Leenhoff's manuscript register of Manet's works (B. N. Estampes, Yb³ 4649) and the Lochard photographs. Normally, the register numbers also appear on the photographs. However, the mounted Lochard photographs which are numbered *309* show the London picture (32, Fig.60), whereas the register entry No.309 describes the final, Mannheim picture (37, Fig.71), '*Signé et daté 19 juin 1867 | cadre ancien | non photographié*'. There is no register entry for the London picture, and no early photograph is known of the Mannheim painting. See Bibliography.

53 See TABARANT [1947], p.141. Lejosne was the original owner of the Courtauld version of *Le déjeuner sur l'herbe* (24, Fig.50).

54 Brown University, *op. cit.*, p.190, No.28.

55 '. . . *le peloton commandé pour l'exécution de l'empereur . . . se compose de six soldats, d'un caporal et d'un officier. Les soldats ont des visages hideux et*

sinistres. Leur uniforme ressemble à l'uniforme français: le képi et la tunique paraissent être en toile grise, le ceinturon en cuir blanc; le pantalon descendant jusqu'aux pieds est d'une étoffe plus foncée. Le caporal, celui qui a achevé Maximilien, est très joli garçon; il a un air "bon enfant" qui contraste singulièrement avec la lugubre besogne dont il a été chargé. Le plus curieux des sept (sic) *est l'officier commandant le peloton; il ne doit pas avoir dix-huit ans.*' Brown University, *op. cit.*, p.120.

56 Brown University, *op. cit.*, p.121.

57 Brown University, *op. cit.*, p.183, No.21.

58 First noticed and discussed by FONSMARK [1984].

59 Kindly made available by The National Gallery, London, with the authorisation of the Director of the Ny Carlsberg Glyptotek in Copenhagen.

60 Brown University, *op. cit.*, p.182, No.19.

61 The X-radiograph of this very large canvas extends right to the edges of the canvas only on one side, where it shows a change of tone over the stretcher at the top. It is reproduced by courtesy of the Doerner Institute, Munich.

62 The paint surface had suggested to several writers, even before the new evidence of the Mannheim X-radiograph, that the officer might originally have been present on the canvas.

63 The face in its final form evokes not so much Mejía's true likeness (see Fig.64, and Brown University, *op. cit.*, p.183, No.20), as images such as Plate 2 of Goya's *Disasters of War*. In addition, all reports mentioned his small stature.

64 Brown University, *op. cit.*, pp.121–22: '. . . *le peuple témoignait ouvertement de sa sympathie et de son indignation. Aucun homme des classes supérieures ne se montrait. La foule était principalement composée de pauvres Indiens et de dames manifestant leurs sympathies sans aucune crainte. . . . Derrière les prisonniers, plus haut sur la colline, se tenait le peuple, presque tous de pauvres Indiens.*'

65 See the exh. cat. Paris/New York [1983], App. II. pp.529–31.

66 I would like to thank Huguette Berès for drawing my attention to this document which has never been published, whereas the handbill was reproduced in Bazire's biography of Manet [1884], p.58.

67 See the exh. cat. Paris/New York [1983], No.124.

68 See note 22 above.

69 See the plan of Manet's Paris in the exh. cat. Paris/New York [1983], pp.502–03.

70 See the account of Fervacques, in MOREAU-NELATON [1926], II, pp.8–9.

71 The date is known from one of the rare proofs which has a design by Bertall dated February 1874 on the verso. See the exh. cat. Ingelheim-am-Rhein [1977], Addenda, No.64; Paris/New York [1983], No.168.

72 The evidence is both extensive and detailed (BOMFORD AND ROY [1983] on the London picture, GIFFORD [1984/85] on the Baltimore canvas, and a recent, unpublished study of the Paris canvas), but also incomplete (the Winterthur picture has not been fully examined or X-radiographed). It is simplified and used selectively in this inevitably tentative account.

I am deeply indebted to Melanie Gifford in Baltimore, to David Bomford at the National Gallery and Robert Bruce-Gardiner at the Courtauld Institute in London for discussing their research, both published and unpublished and for helping in many ways with the investigation presented here.

73 Records are scarce for the years immediately following the war and the Commune, and it is not until the 1880s that the official *Bottins* (annual directories) and regular advertisements in the press present a full and clear picture of Parisian places of entertainment.

74 Léon's annotations on the photograph card give a date of 1877 (under which the London picture was catalogued in the 1884 exhibition), despite the signature and date 1879 recorded on the canvas. The register description is: *Signé et daté 1879. Moitié* [over *Partie*] *d'un tableau qui se trouve à Marseille. On aperçoit la silhouette de Goeneutte. Le chapeau gris de Manet s'aperçoit. La fille est la servante de la Brasserie Reichshoffen sur le Boulevard Rochechouart. C'est* [struck out] *l'idée vient* [or *tient*] *de cet endroit.*

The photograph card is inscribed at upper right *1877* (in ink over pencil), and at top centre *Signé Manet 1879*; then comes the number *8* (above the Lochard photograph), which corresponds with the register number, the pencil note *fait pendant à Reischoffen app[artient] à M. Barroil Marseille*; below the title: *La servante de bocks*, is a long pen and ink inscription: *Peint dans l'atelier de la rue de St Pétersbourg d'après des croquis pris à la brasserie Reichshoffen du Boulevard Rochechouart. Moitié d'une grande toile. L'autre pendant représente assis à la table Henri Guérard, graveur, et Ellen Andrée. Le chapeau gris est celui d'Edouard Manet. La servante est celle qui servait à la Brasserie.*

75 In which he worked between July 1872 and July 1878, when he was obliged to move for a few months to the studio of the Swedish artist Rosen, at 70 rue d'Amsterdam, see note 69.

76 In the 1884 memorial exhibition catalogue, the London picture appears as No.88, among the paintings of 1877, and a note in the draft project for the exhibition made by Edmond Bazire (Manet's first biographer) records, under 1877, that *Reischofen* (sic) *à M. Barroil de Marseille n'a pas été exposé*. See the ms. *Copie pour Moreau-Nélaton . . .* , p.[104]. These documents serve to correct the statement by Tabarant, who based so much of his writing on Manet's life and art on documents in his possession (now in the Pierpont

Morgan Library, New York), that the original, large *Reichshoffen* composition was painted in Rosen's studio on the rue d'Amsterdam, that is, between July 1878 and April 1879. Tabarant seems to have confused the start of the project with Manet's reworking of the cut canvases in the new studio.

77 The date of this particular engraving was recorded as November 1872 by Paul Blondel who formed the remarkable collection of topographical cuttings, now in the Bibliothèque Nationale. It therefore affords a much earlier date for the Hanlon Lees' performances than that cited in the exh. cat. Paris/New York [1983], No.172.

78 The same is true of the figure of Edmond André, in the Baltimore café picture (**54**, Fig.94, Col. ill.6), whose head was virtually the only part of that canvas to escape extensive repainting.

79 She had been painted by Manet at her easel (National Gallery, London; RW 154), and he sent her many letters during the siege of Paris, and also wrote to her after her marriage. See the exh. cat. Paris [1978], Nos.107, 108.

80 See the drypoint by Desboutin; see G. DE KNYFF: *L'Art Libre au XIXe Siècle ou La Vie de Norbert Goeneutte*, Paris [1978], p.4.

81 See notes 74 and 99.

82 DURET [1902], pp.107–08; MOREAU-NELATON [1926], II, p.52.

83 See the technical summary, pp.84–85.

84 See the *Copie pour Moreau Nélaton . . . , op. cit.*, p.[79].

85 PROUST [1897], p.311; TABARANT [1931], p.333.

86 Barroil's picture was of course never further reworked, and when Bazire noted its absence from the 1884 exhibition, he referred to it by the old title *Reichshoffen*. See notes 74 and 76.

87 Although Manet's surviving drawings are extremely fragmentary, it is perhaps significant that a high proportion is related to paintings.

88 The combination of figures all facing in different directions, in the fragment from (a) to (1), suggests a possible connection with the Baltimore café picture (**54**, Fig.94, Col. ill.6), for which no source has yet been proposed.

89 Although Manet frequently included cut-off figures in his compositions, such as the figures at the left and right edges respectively of the Winterthur and Baltimore canvases (**45** and **54**, Figs.81, 94, Col. ills.4, 6), the dancer on stage in the Paris picture (**49**, Fig.85, Col. ill.7), or the officer at the right edge of the first version of the *Execution of Maximilian* in Boston (**31**, Fig.57), these were figures clearly cut through (cut in half, in the case of the dancer) and not simply trimmed or shaved by the edge of the canvas.

90 Permission was generously given and arrangements made to examine the Paris *Serveuse de bocks* in the Louvre; the edging paper was removed, paint samples were taken, and the canvas was X-radiographed. The interest and cooperation of Segolène Bergeon and Annick Lautraite in the Atelier de Restoration and of Lola Faillant-Dumas in the Laboratoire de Recherche des Musées de France were instrumental in carrying out this examination, and the results of the pigment analysis carried out by Jean-Paul Rioux in the Laboratoire will be published later.

91 See BOMFORD AND ROY [1983], pp.6–8.

92 See RW 275 and 288; *Copie pour Moreau-Nélaton . . . , op. cit.*, p.[76].

93 There is a current debate as to whether what have generally been called transfer lithographs (or autographies) are in fact reproductive *gillotage* prints.

The relationship between these two closely related drawings affords an insight into Manet's reworking of individual motifs: the boy wearing a cap, in the foreground in the notebook sketch, was not originally present; the pencil sketch describes only the vague shape that appears in the ink wash drawing, and Manet subsequently 'completed' the pencil outline with black chalk on the notebook page, but left the wash drawing untouched.

94 Paint splashes which might have provided interesting samples for analysis and comparison with the London picture were at some stage removed from the surface of the sheet.

95 Lochard photograph No.187, *Croquis d'une chanteuse de café aux Champs-Elysées – dessiné sur papier jaune* (Bernheim-Jeune archives, Paris, Lochard album 3, p.174, see Fig.90; Morgan Library, New York, Lochard album 2, p.75; RW II 512) and No.188, *Croquis dessiné sur papier jaune / Chanteuse de café-concert aux Champs-Elysées* (B. N. Estampes, Dc300h, p.65; Bernheim-Jeune archives, album 4, p.253; see Fig.91). This second drawing, RW II 514, has disappeared since the 1884 sale of Manet's studio when it was acquired by Duret.

96 Since the drawing is on 'yellow paper', like the ink wash version of the same orchestra players (Fig.87), it is probably a variant of the drawing that was used for the print.

97 RW II 504, 505, 511, 515, 519–21 and 526.

98 See RW II 526 (pencil sketch) and Leiris 486, Fig.368 (ink drawing, reproduced in *La Vie Moderne* [17th April 1880], p.257).

The 'café-concert on the Champs-Elysées' was also the subject of a painting (RW 310, see also RW 309) which shows a singer on a stage in a garden setting, and a view onto the prompter's box-cum-music stand, with the conductor waving his baton. For a painting directly based on Manet's sketches, the *Chanteuse de café-concert* (RW 281), and the tambourine painted for Antonin Proust with the same singer and orchestra motif (RW 322); see the exh. cat. Paris [1978], No.18, Col. ill. And on a tiny canvas, said to bear Manet's signature on the verso, the little trombonist from the orchestra appears, in

front of the stage and prompter's box, but immediately behind the figures of Ellen Andrée and Guérard from the Winterthur picture (RW 279).

99 This would account for the raising of the foreground hand with a pipe, to obscure a profile view of the man in 'Manet's grey hat', who must previously have looked across the table as he talked with Guérard – now in the Winterthur canvas (**42** and **47**, Figs. 77, 83). See the technical summary on p.84).

100 . . . *de nouveau, chaque fois, n'étant autre que tous sans rester different, à volonté. . . . l'immédiate fraîcheur de la rencontre. . . .* S. MALLARMÉ: *Divagations*, Paris [1897], p.128; *Œuvres complètes*, ed. Pléiade, Paris [1974], p.532.

101 I.e., before the lower edge was trimmed away and before Manet cut the canvas through the centre of the table (trimming off the edge of the *M* of *Manet* – see BOMFORD AND ROY [1983], p.13).

102 *La Vie Moderne* [8th May 1880], pp.303, 304.

103 Another drawing, in watercolour with pen and sepia ink touches, was recently acquired by the Musée d'Orsay (Louvre, Cabinet des Dessins, RF 38.945). It belonged to Jacques-Émile Blanche, but its condition and the cutting of the signature make it difficult to judge in relation to the painting and drawing discussed here. See *Catalogue sommaire illustré des nouvelles acquisitions du Musée d'Orsay* [1983], No.142.

104 Musée des Beaux-Arts, Tournai. RW 291.

105 See the Register of Manet's works, *op. cit.*, No.265.

106 Engraving from an unidentified journal in the Blondel topographical collection, B. N. Estampes (Va 286, vol.13, H 71016).

107 *Que demande l'étranger en arrivant à Paris? – Les Folies-Bergère. – C'est que là surtout se trouve condensé l'esprit du crû. On y voit les habitudes parisiennes comme en deshabillé; on y vit de la vie de ce monde léger, aimable, prime-sautier, charmant, poli, étincelant de brio et finement moqueur, dont M. Sari a si heureusement saisi les goûts. . . . L'esprit parisien se condense et se respire dans cette atmosphere tiède et parfumée; mais on comprend aussi que ce lieu de délices, tout à la fois théâtre, concert, café, jardin, est également créé en vue de la foule cosmopolite. . . .*

Partout des comptoirs . . . tenus par de charmantes vendeuses, dont les yeux espiègles et les gracieux sourires attirent une foule de clients. L'enchanteur, M. Sari, a semé dans son jardin fantastique toutes les séductions. La troupe des Hanlon-Lees, des pantomimes, des ballets, une musique entrainante . . . rien n'est négligé pour varier les plaisirs. Le regard est ravi, l'oreille charmée, tout vous séduit, vous éblouit.

Cutting from an unidentified journal in the Blondel topographical collection, B. N. Estampes (Va 286, vol.13, H 71021).

108 Register No.247. *Dessin à la plume fait d'après des croquis pris aux Folies-Bergère*, Bernheim-Jeune archives, Paris, Lochard album 3, p.203; see Fig.97. Leiris 517.

Two other drawings (mounted together, Register No.249) are described on the Lochard photograph as *Scènes prises aux Folies-Bergère*, Bernheim-Jeune archives, Lochard albums 3 and 5, p.201; Morgan Library, New York, album 2, p.72. RW 520 and 521.

109 *Esquisse du Bar aux Folies-Bergère. Première idée du tableau. C'est le bar au premier étage à droite de la scène et d'avant-scène. Portrait de Dupray. A été peint dans l'été 1881*. B. N. Estampes (Yb³ 4649, No.265).

110 *Peint d'après des croquis pris aux Folies-Bergère. Henri du Pray cause avec la fille du comptoir dans l'atelier de la rue d'Amsterdam.* Bernheim-Jeune archives, Paris, Lochard albums 1 and 6, p.50; Morgan Library, New York, Lochard album 1, p.33.

111 Engraving in the Blondel topographical collections, B. N. Estampes (Va 287, vol.13, H.71019).

112 See note 108.

113 The facilities kindly afforded by Rini Dippl, curator at the Stedelijk Museum, for the examination of the picture, and the possibility of discussing it with the museum's restoration staff, enabled many new features to be seen and assessed, and we are indebted to Rini Dippl for arranging for the X-radiograph to be made.

114 The composition must have been even more unbalanced when the canvas extended farther to the left.

115 The Director of the Courtauld Institute Galleries, Dennis Farr, kindly agreed that a new X-radiograph should be made (since the previous X-ray image was obscured by the cross-bracing of the stretcher). Robert Bruce-Gardiner was responsible for obtaining an outstandingly clear and readable X-radiograph in the Technology Department of the Courtauld Institute.

116 Register No.138; Lochard photograph in B. N. Estampes (Dc300h, p.49) and Bernheim-Jeune archives, Paris, Lochard albums 4 and 8, p.274.

117 See F. CACHIN in the exh. cat. Paris/New York [1983], No.211.

118 PROUST [1897], p.311.

119 J. JEANNIOT, in MOREAU-NELATON [1926], II, p.95.

120 *La musique aux Tuileries* (National Gallery, London). RW 51.

121 See note 116.

122 This tiny image reproduces a portrait sketch (Private collection, Paris, RW 374). Jeanne was also the model, as *Le Printemps* (Private collection, New York, RW 372), with Méry Laurent as *L'Automne* (Musée des Beaux Arts, Nancy, RW 393), for an unfinished series of the four seasons that Manet was painting for Antonin Proust.

Exhibition checklist

The French titles are normally contemporary, documented titles. In a few instances, customary titles have been retained. Dimensions are in centimetres, height by width. The indication 'inscribed' rather than 'signed', denotes a signature that is not autograph. The studio stamp (red intials *E.M*, stamped on the works in Manet's studio at his death) is mentioned where present.

Hors d'Œuvre

I.a. X-radiograph of **II**. *Still-life with a ham*.

The X-ray films reveal the many changes made to this deceptively straightforward-looking picture. Manet painted out a fruit or vegetable in the right foreground and one or more objects in the background to the right. He also altered the shape of the dish and changed the folds in the tablecloth, painting over the one which shows under the centre of the knife blade.

I.b. Positive X-ray print from **I.a**. (Fig.18.)

II. *Le jambon (The ham)*. c.1875–78.
Oil on canvas. 32.4 by 41.2 cm. Signed l.r. *Manet*.
The Burrell Collection, Glasgow Museums and Art Galleries (35.308).

This splendid ham on a silver dish, set off against a white tablecloth and dark, patterned background, owes much of its impact as a 'close-up' image to the facts that it was cut from a larger canvas and that Manet radically simplified its presentation. X-rays show that apart from the ham itself, the entire picture surface was repainted. The cut canvas was put onto a smaller stretcher and the painted surface now wraps around the sides of the present stretcher. Cracks in the paint surface at upper and lower right hint at over-painted objects beneath. (Fig.19.)

Bathers and Picnics – The Early Nudes

1. Sketch for *La nymphe surprise (The surprised nymph)*. c.1858–60.
Oil on panel. 35.5 by 46cm. Inscribed l.r. *E.Manet*.
Nasjonalgalleriet, Oslo (1182).

This composition sketch, for a large painting of *Moses saved from the waters* or a *Surprised nymph* of which only a fragment survives (see **15** and **16**), was painted over a reclining nude which appears in the X-ray image (**2**). Sandpaper was used to efface the nude on the mahogany panel, and the later composition sketch was freely painted over the disturbed surface. (Fig.20, Col.ill.3.)

2.a. X-radiograph of **1**. *Reclining nude (Danaë?)*. c.1857–58.

The X-ray image of **1** shows, beneath the composition sketch with a nude bather in a landscape, traces of a reclining nude. The figure was almost obliterated, but the outlines and actual size correspond very closely with those of a red chalk study of a nude (**25**), and also with Titian's *Danaë* in Naples (see Fig.52a). On a similar wood panel, Manet copied Titian's *Venus of Urbino* in Florence (**28**).

2.b. Positive X-ray print from **2.a**. (Fig.21.)

3. *The finding of Moses*. c.1858–60.
Pen and sepia ink with wash, over pencil, squared in red chalk.
Smooth laid paper, watermark *JOYNSON*. 33.3 by 28 cm.
Studio stamp l.r.
Museum Boymans-van Beuningen, Rotterdam (F II 105).

In this drawing, the kneeling woman is drawn on a page from a notebook, and the composition has been extended on strips of the same paper added on the right and at the bottom. The 'Moses' motif relates the drawing to the composition sketch once identified as *Moses saved from the waters* (**1**). (Fig.24.)

4. *Bathsheba*, after Giulio Romano. c.1858–60.
Pencil on smooth laid paper. 17.8 by 13.2 cm. Studio stamp l.r.
Cabinet des Dessins, Musée du Louvre, Paris (RF 11.970).

In this drawing Manet copied part of a ceiling design by Giulio Romano in the Palazzo del Tè at Mantua. The reversed composition suggests that Manet copied the design from a French seventeenth-century engraving (**5**) and not from the original ceiling in Mantua. (Fig.25.)

5. *David spying upon Bathsheba*, by J. Corneille le Jeune after Giulio Romano.
Engraving. 26 by 26 cm. Inscribed *Vidit David mulierem se lavantem*.
Cabinet des Estampes, Bibliothèque Nationale, Paris (Bb 14).

The first in a set of three prints (with a frontispiece) depicting the story of Bathsheba, and engraved from drawings made by Jean-Baptiste Corneille in the palace at Mantua. The engraving is inscribed with the Latin quotation from the Book of Samuel, ch.IX, v.2: 'David saw a woman washing herself'. One of the several sets in the Bibliothèque Nationale belonged to Devéria who was a 'friend and protector' of the young Manet. (Fig.26.)

6. *The toilet of Bathsheba*, by J. Corneille le Jeune after Giulio Romano.
Engraving. 26 by 26 cm. Inscribed *Nuntiatumque est ei quod ipsa esset Bethsabee*.
Cabinet des Estampes, Bibliothèque Nationale, Paris (Bb 14).

The second print in the series (see **5**) shows Bathsheba attended by her maidservants, and the Biblical inscription reads on from the first: 'And he sent to ask whether this was Bathsheba'. The composition is related to Manet's studies of a woman at her toilet (**10–14**) and he evidently responded to the bold and vigorous forms of Giulio's designs. (Fig.27.)

7. *Susannah and the elders*, by Lucas Vorstermann after Rubens.
Engraving. 39 by 27.8 cm.
Department of Prints and Drawings, the British Museum, London (1981.u.372).

The pose of the startled nude in this reversed engraving after a lost painting by Rubens is very close to Manet's *Nymphe surprise* (**1** and **15**). (Fig.30 has been reversed.)

8. *Seated bather, facing right (I)*. c.1858–60.
Pen and sepia ink with wash over traces of red chalk. On thin wove
paper. 26.7 by 19.9 cm.
Museum Boymans-van Beuningen, Rotterdam (F II 191).

This drawing is so close to another, very well known sheet (**9**) that
previously it has been only attributed to Manet. However, its identical
technical characteristics and similar (though less accomplished handling)
must confirm the attribution. (Fig. 33.)

9. *Seated bather, facing right (II)*. c.1858–60.
Pen and sepia ink with wash, over red chalk, with corrections in black
chalk. On thin wove paper. 26.5 by 20.4 cm. Studio stamp l.r.
Private collection, London.

In this powerful, Rembrandtesque drawing, Manet evokes the opulent
forms of his Dutch friend, Suzanne Leenhoff. The young woman gave
piano lessons to the Manet brothers and was married to the artist in
1863. The wash drawing was no doubt made in connection with the
Nymphe surprise (**1** and **15**). The nude's right arm, originally lying
between her thighs, is corrected in black chalk so that it lies across her
stomach. The drawing was bought by Degas at the 1884 sale of the
contents of Manet's studio. (Fig. 34.)

10. *Seated bather, with both arms raised*. c.1858–60.
Red chalk with lead pencil corrections, squared in pencil. On laid
paper, watermark *NF*. 30.9 by 25.5 cm. Studio stamp centre r.
Cabinet des Estampes, Bibliothèque Nationale, Paris (No. 8).

This handsome study, in exceptionally fresh condition, is squared with
lines drawn to help Manet transfer the figure, on a larger scale, onto
canvas. No painting is known, but the figure may lurk, unsuspected,
beneath another composition. (Fig. 35.)

11. *Seated bather, with left arm raised*. c.1858–60.
Red chalk on laid paper, watermark *NF*. 26.6 by 23 cm. Signed l.r.
E.Manet.
The Art Institute of Chicago (1967.30).

In this drawing, the seated nude holds up her long locks which a
maidservant is dressing, as in the *Nymphe surprise* composition (see **1**
and **15**). The attendant looming directly behind the nude appears to
have been suppressed when a second attendant, with a loosely
suggested garment over her arm, was drawn in further to the left. This
figure is very close to the one which appears in the etching and its
preparatory drawing (**13** and **14**). (Fig. 36, Col. ill. 1.)

12. *Tracing of* **11**. *Seated bather, with left arm raised*. c.1858–60.
Incised 'mica' sheet, with black chalk touches. 23.7 by 15.9 cm. Incised
initials l.r. on seat. Studio stamp l.r.
Cabinet des Dessins, Musée du Louvre, Paris (RF 30.401).

This very brittle and damaged sheet of thin, transparent material is
unique in Manet's œuvre. It shows one of the tracing methods he used
to rework his designs onto other supports or in different formats. The
outlines of the nude in the Chicago drawing (**11**), which are incised on
this mica sheet, were probably used as a stage in the preparation of
La toilette, seen here in an etching and its preparatory drawing (**13** and
14). This composition was probably the subject of a lost or still
'hidden' painting. (Fig. 37.)

13. *La toilette*. c.1860–61.
Red chalk on laid paper, watermark *NF*. 29.1 by 21 cm.
The Home House Trustees, Courtauld Institute Galleries, London.

This drawing was made in preparation for an etching (**14**) and was
incised (the paper is cut through in places) for transfer to the
copperplate. Since the design of the drawing was marked directly, and
not reversed on the plate, it appears in reverse in the print. The
summary lines of the drawing show the bather and her attendant
developed from the Chicago composition (**11**). The 'framing' lines
suggest that if a painting existed, Manet was trying out a new format
with a view to cutting his canvas. (Fig. 38.)

14. *La toilette*. c.1860–61.
Etching. 28.7 by 22.5 cm. Initial *M* l.r.
Department of Prints and Drawings, British Museum, London
(1949.4.11.2563).

The etching was published in 1862, with the title *La toilette*. The
complex interior scene strongly suggests that it was based on a
painting which Manet may have cut down (see **13**) or over-painted. No
direct source for the subject has been found, but it appears to be of
Italian renaissance inspiration. (Fig. 39.)

15. 1872 photograph by Godet of *La nymphe surprise*.
32 by 26 cm.
Cabinet des Estampes, Bibliothèque Nationale, Paris (Dc 300a, II).

This early photographic print was made by Godet in 1872. It shows
the canvas cut from a large work – based on the oil sketch (**1**) – and
repainted by Manet before he sent it to an exhibition in St Petersburg
(Leningrad) in 1861. In the exhibition, the picture was entitled *Nymph
and satyr*. Godet's photograph shows the satyr's head which can just
be made out among the branches, in the upper right corner. The head
was removed at an unknown date after Manet's death. X-rays of the
painting (**16**) show how Manet altered the cut canvas. (Fig. 40.)

16. X-radiograph of *La nymphe surprise* (see **15**).
Photographic print from the composite X-radiograph of the large
painting, 146 by 114 cm., now in the Museo Nacional de Bellas Artes,
Buenos Aires (2712).

The X-ray image shows the areas that Manet painted out after he had
cut the figure of the bather from his large painting (see **15**). At the left
edge is part of the woman who is seen from the back in the Oslo
composition sketch (**1**). Behind the nude, the attendant who combs her
hair (as in the oil sketch, but placed further to the right) appears very
clearly and has a remarkably beautiful face. There is no trace in the
X-rays of the very thinly painted satyr's head, which Manet added
before sending the painting to an exhibition in Russia in 1861. (Fig. 41.)

17. Photograph of Titian's *Venus del Pardo* (formerly called *Jupiter and
Antiope*; Musée du Louvre, Paris, INV 752), by Alinari, c.1890–1900.
18 by 23.5 cm.
Documentation du Département des Peintures, Musée du Louvre,
Paris.

This photograph, taken after Manet's death, shows Titian's very large
picture hanging at eye level (above a marbled dado, with an iron
barrier rail), as Manet may have seen it in the Grande Galerie in the
1850s and 1860s. (Fig. 42.)

18. X-radiograph of **19**. *Le déjeuner sur l'herbe*.

The X-ray image shows the wide, open landscape to the left, with
slender trees behind the figures. There are plants and grasses in place
of the hat and dress in the left foreground. To the left of the seated
nude is a partially scraped form which may have been a hunting dog
similar to those in Titian's *Venus del Pardo*, which is the closest source
for the landscape (see **17** and **20**). The figure group shows signs of
considerable repainting, particularly in the nude's body and the head
of the man behind her, but was always close to its source in the
Marcantonio engraving after Raphael (**21**). The unclothed woman
seated on drapery in the company of two fully-dressed young men is a
reinterpretation of the picture known as *Pastorale* or *Le concert
champêtre* in the Louvre, then attributed to Giorgione (see **22**). (Fig. 44.)

19. Photograph of *Le déjeuner sur l'herbe*. Dated 1863.
Oil on canvas. 208 by 264 cm. (originally 214 by 270 cm.). Signed and
dated l.r. *ed. Manet 1863*.
Musée d'Orsay – Galeries du Jeu de Paume, Paris (RF 1668).

This is the final state of the painting. Heavy tree-trunks and foliage
obscure the underlying landscape, seen in the X-ray image (**18**), as
they do in the earlier *Nymphe surprise* (**15** and **16**). The straw hat and
spotted muslin dress have been added on the ground beside the picnic
objects, stressing that the girl is not a 'nude' but a woman who has
taken off her clothes. (Fig. 45.)

20. *Jupiter amoureux d'Antiope se transforme en Satire*, by Bernard Baron after Titian's *Venus del Pardo* (see **17**).
Engraving. 38.7 by 66.3 cm. (reversed composition).
Department of Prints and Drawings, British Museum, London (1855.6.9.224).

This is one of the largest engravings – on a double page – in the *recueil* Crozat, a splendid eighteenth-century publication of reproductive prints after the finest paintings and drawings in French collections. (Fig. 46.)

21. *The judgment of Paris*, by Marcantonio Raimondi after Raphael.
Engraving. 29.5 by 44.3 cm.
Department of Prints and Drawings, British Museum, London (1973.u.9).

This is a particularly fine, early impression of a famous print which Manet could have seen in the Bibliothèque Nationale (then Impériale) or other collections in Paris. He used the seated group of two river gods and a water nymph for the *Déjeuner sur l'herbe*, painted for the Salon of 1863 and shown in the famous Salon des Refusés (**19**). But although his models took up the same poses in his studio, the male figures were dressed, as they are in the *Pastorale* or *Concert champêtre*, then attributed to Giorgione (see **22**). (Fig. 47.)

22. *Pastorale*, by Nicolas Dupuy after Giorgione (now known as *Le concert champêtre*, and attributed to Titian; Musée du Louvre, Paris, INV 71).
Engraving. 33 by 38.5 cm.
Department of Prints and Drawings, British Museum, London (1855.6.9.219).

Manet's life-long friend, Antonin Proust, recorded a conversation which confirms that the *Déjeuner sur l'herbe* (**19**) was based on this famous painting in the Louvre, then attributed to Giorgione. Manet said that he had copied the painting as a student and that it had grown dark with time; he wanted to reinterpret it in natural light, as a scene of modern life. The engraving published in the *recueil* Crozat (see **20**) shows the composition in reverse and in this form it is more closely related to the figures in the *Déjeuner sur l'herbe* than the original painting in the Louvre. (Fig. 48.)

23. *Le déjeuner sur l'herbe*. c. 1863–65.
Pen and ink and water-colour over lead pencil. On laid paper, watermark *J WHATMAN*. 40.8 by 48 cm.
The Visitors of the Ashmolean Museum, Oxford (1980.83).
[Original drawing on show for only part of the exhibition.]

This water-colour drawing was probably based on a tracing from a photograph of Manet's great painting (**19**). It cannot have been made as a composition sketch, since it reflects the final design of the painting, rather than the earlier, underlying composition seen in the X-ray image (**18**). It may have been made as a preparatory study for an etching which Manet either never began or of which no proofs have survived. It was probably made before he painted the smaller picture (**24**), and may be closely connected with the development of that slightly different composition. (Fig. 49.)

24. *Le déjeuner sur l'herbe*. c. 1864–68?
Oil on canvas. 89.5 by 116 cm. Signed l.l. *Manet*.
The Home House Trustees, Courtauld Institute Galleries, London.

This reduced version of Manet's large Salon painting (**19**) is said to have been painted for his friend, the Commandant Lejosne. Being a 'replica' of an existing composition, its style is unusual and rather difficult to date. Slight but significant alterations in the composition, which tend to give it greater stability and coherence, suggest that it was painted at a later date than the large picture. (Fig. 50.)

25. *Reclining nude*. c. 1857–59.
Red chalk on paid paper (watermark *NF*?). 24.7 by 45.7 cm. Studio stamp below the knees.
Cabinet des Dessins, Musée du Louvre, Paris (RF 24.335).

This drawing, hitherto thought to be a study for *Olympia*, was probably made in connection with a much earlier painting. The outlines of the figure correspond in size and shape with what one can see of the reclining nude under the composition sketch for the *Nymphe surprise* (see **1** and **2**), and the pose of the figure is related to representations of *Danaë* (see **27**). (Fig. 51.)

26. *Reclining nude*. c. 1857–59.
Red chalk, squared. On laid paper, watermark *NF*. 22.5 by 30 cm.
Cabinet des Estampes, Bibliothèque Nationale, Paris (No. 7).

This study, squared for transfer to canvas, is closely related to the larger drawing in the Louvre (**25**). The drapery over the nude's thighs recalls Titian's *Danaë* painting in Naples (Fig. 52a), which may have been the model for the figure seen in the X-ray of the *Nymphe surprise* sketch (**2**). If the figure was transferred to a large canvas, she was a direct forerunner of *Olympia* (**30**). (Fig. 52.)

27. *Danaë*, by Louis Desplaces after Titian (Hermitage Museum, Leningrad).
Engraving. 25.5 by 33 cm.
Department of Prints and Drawings, British Museum, London (1855.6.9.227).

This engraving from the *recueil* Crozat (see **20**) is a reversed copy of the version of Titian's composition in Pierre Crozat's own collection (now in the Hermitage, Leningrad). It shows Danaë on her bed, with Jupiter in the form of a shower of gold coins which an old woman is catching in her apron. (Fig. 53 has been reversed to conform with the original painting.)

28. Photograph of the *Venus of Urbino*, by Manet after Titian (Galleria degli Uffizi, Florence). 1857?
Oil on panel. 24 by 37 cm.
Private collection.

This small painting was probably made by Manet during his visit to Florence in the winter of 1857. Like the mahogany panel on which he painted a reclining nude (see **2**), later erased and replaced by the sketch for the *Nymphe surprise* (**1**), this would have formed part of the artist's travelling kit. Drawn and painted records of masterpieces of Italian art, which Manet saw on his journey to Italy or studied in Paris, were among the most important influences on the development of his art. (Fig. 54.)

29. X-radiograph of **30**. *Olympia*.

The X-ray image shows the outline of the tied-back curtain to the left of the black attendant, and the view through into a light area behind her. This area, particularly to the right, appears to have been very strongly scraped and it is difficult to make out the original design. It must have corresponded to the view of the room in Titian's *Venus of Urbino* (see **28**). The paper round the bouquet was later extended (the maid's dress shows clearly beneath it), many alterations were made to the end of the bed and the draperies generally, and the nude's head shows signs of much scraping and repainting. (Fig. 55.)

30. Photograph of *Olympia*. Signed and dated 1863.
Oil on canvas, 130.5 by 190 cm.
Musée d'Orsay – Galeries du Jeu de Paume, Paris (RF 644).

Manet's first masterpiece was developed through earlier versions (see **25**, **26** and **28**) and directly on the canvas. It may have been painted over a fairly long period, since the X-ray image (**29**) shows signs of extensive reworking. The final design, with its confined space and the emphasis on the unseen admirer's bouquet presented to Olympia, brings the viewer into a dramatically close encounter with the nude on the bed. All the elements which establish the 'modernity' of this image, in particular the slippers, the outsize bouquet and the cat, appear to have been added when Manet was completing his painting. (Fig. 56.)

The Execution of Maximilian

31. Photograph of *The execution of Maximilian* – First version. 1867.
Oil on canvas. 196 by 259.8 cm.
Museum of Fine Arts, Boston (30.444).

This canvas is a first, full-scale draft of the execution composition that Manet reworked in two further large designs (**32** and **37**). It shows the Emperor Maximilian standing upright on the left, wearing a Mexican sombrero, and one of his generals struck by the shots from the firing squad's muskets. The design is roughly sketched-in and is confused in many areas, particularly in the soldiers' heads where the sombreros have been partially transformed into military *képis*, as is clear in the X-ray image (**31a**). (Fig. 57.)

31a. X-radiograph of **31**. *The execution of Maximilian* – First version.

The X-ray image of the thinly painted canvas is difficult to interpret, particularly on the left. It does, however, show that there were no major changes in the firing squad, beyond the transformation of the wide sombreros into *képis*, and that the soldier with his rifle and officer with a sword on the right were originally in the same positions. (Fig. 58.)

32. Photograph by Lochard c.1883 of *The execution of Maximilian* – Second version (1867–68).
Enlargement from an original photographic print (9 by 6 cm.).
Cabinet des Estampes, Bibliothèque Nationale, Paris (Dc 300g, I).

This enlargement from a small and unevenly faded photographic print shows the second version of Manet's *Maximilian* composition as it appeared shortly after the artist's death. The left side of the canvas had already been damaged and cut off, so that only General Miramón, clasping the Emperor's left hand, is visible. The painting suffered further damage and four fragments were saved from the large canvas. They were reunited by Degas and are now in the National Gallery, London. (Fig. 60.)

33. X-radiograph of **35**. Composition sketch of *The execution of Maximilian* – Intermediate design. 1868.

This X-ray image shows the composition sketch as painted when Manet decided to rework his *Maximilian* design. This was probably after completing the second version (**32**), now in the National Gallery, London. It is a complex image because of the many changes made in the course of work. The principal ones affect the group of victims and the setting. The most obvious alteration, when compared to the final state of the sketch (**35**), is the Emperor's sombrero which is here placed horizontally, as it is in both the first large version in Boston (**31**) and in the lithograph (**34**). The victims' legs and feet are also seen in the same positions as in the lithograph, while General Mejía, on the left, is in much the same position as in the Boston painting (**31**), with his head falling forward. (Fig. 67.)

34. *The execution of Maximilian*. 1868.
Lithograph. 33.3 by 43.3 cm. Signed l.l. *Manet*. Impression from the only edition, published 1884.
Department of Prints and Drawings, British Museum, London (1913.8.14.55).

Manet prepared his lithograph, intending to publish it to coincide with the showing of his final painting of the *Execution of Maximilian* at the Salon of 1869. He was advised that the canvas would be refused and that publication of the lithograph would not be authorised. His printer, Lemercier, even wanted to destroy the design on the lithographic stone, but Manet raised the issue of an artist's freedom of expression, and the stone was finally returned to him.

   The lithograph is close to the design of the early, underlying version of the Copenhagen sketch seen in the X-ray (**33**). It shows signs of changes in the composition, particularly in the placing of the wall, which confirm that it was probably made between the two stages of the oil sketch (**33** and **35**). (Fig. 68.)

35. Sketch for *The execution of Maximilian*. 1868–69/1879?
Oil on canvas. 50 by 60 cm. Signed and dated l.l. *Manet 1867*.
Ny Carlsberg Glyptotek, Copenhagen (924).

The surface of the Copenhagen sketch shows clear evidence of the extensive alterations made to it. Thick paint swirls around the legs and feet of the victims, which were pushed back, away from their position in line with the soldiers (as seen in the X-ray and the lithograph, **33** and **34**). In addition to the throwing back of General Mejía's head (already seen in the lithograph), the Emperor's sombrero has been tilted back so that it forms a halo round his head, and the smoke billows above, rather than below, the musket barrels. The wall now runs straight across the canvas, behind the figures. The picture is squared in pencil (numbers are visible in the squares at the left edge), and the squaring was used to transfer the design to the third and final version of the composition, now in Mannheim (**36** and **37**). (Fig. 69, Col. ill. 10.)

36. X-radiograph of **37**. *The execution of Maximilian* – Third version.

The X-ray image shows that Manet faithfully transposed the final design of the Copenhagen sketch onto his third, large canvas. Apart from the slightly altered appearance of the head of Maximilian, the whole composition of the sketch is reflected in the underlying design of the large painting. General Mejía's head is thrown right back, Maximilian clasps Miramón's hand in the grip seen in the London picture (**32** and Fig. 61), and the commanding officer, later painted out, appears as a ghostly figure between the firing squad and the N.C.O. on the right. It is worth noting that no smoke obscures the lower part of the Emperor's face and beard, suggesting that the smoke which swirls about the victims and against the wall in the final state of the Copenhagen sketch (**35**) and of this painting (**37**) was a later addition. (Fig. 70.)

37. Photograph of *The execution of Maximilian* – Third version.
1868–69/1879?
Oil on canvas. 252 by 305 cm. Signed and dated l.l. *Manet/19 Juin 1867*.
Städtische Kunsthalle, Mannheim (281).

The final state of the third and last of Manet's *Maximilian* compositions shows the picture as it was exhibited in the United States in the winter of 1879–80 (see **38**). The most striking difference with the Copenhagen sketch (**35**) and the underlying, X-ray image of this canvas (**36**) lies in the absence of the commanding officer with his sword raised. He was painted out and replaced by symbolic, almost subliminal touches of red, suggesting his cap and a tassel against the ground below.

   Other alterations include the reworking of Mejía's head, which becomes a more recognisable – and heroic – 'portrait', the retouching of Maximilian's face, the transformation of the clasped hands into an almost formless amalgam of raw flesh, and the refining of the victims' shadows, which emphasises the fragility as well as the cohesion of the group as it faces the firing squad. It is possible that these final changes were not made until the decision to exhibit the picture in America, in 1879. (Fig. 71. Col. ill. 11.)

38. Handbill and announcement for the exhibition of *The execution of Maximilian* (**37**) in the United States.
Private collection.

Emilie Ambre, a singer whom Manet met in the late 1870s, persuaded the artist to let her take the final huge canvas of the *Execution of Maximilian* (**37**) on tour with her in the United States. The small handbill advertises the exhibition of the painting on Broadway, New York, where it was shown at the end of 1879 before going on to Boston.

   The notice gives details of the historical event of the picture 'by the celebrated French painter, E. Manet', describing it 'as being so startling, that its exhibition was formally prohibited' in France. (Fig. 72: handbill.)

39. *La barricade* (recto). Reversed tracing of *The execution of Maximilian* (verso). 1867–68?/1871.
Brush and Indian ink, water-colour and gouache over pencil (recto). Indented lines, partially redrawn in black chalk (verso). On two joined sheets of paper (wove lower half, laid upper half). 46.4 by 32.6 cm. (height of lower sheet 30.5 cm.). Studio stamp l.r. (recto).
Szépmüvészeti Múzeum, Budapest (1935.2734).

The impressive water-colour and gouache drawing of *La barricade* shows the execution of French citizens during the crushing of the Paris Commune in 1871. But beneath this design, clearly visible in the pencil outlines of the figures, is the composition of the *Execution of Maximilian* (**32–37**). On the back of the lower sheet, indented outlines trace the Maximilian composition in reverse, and some of the outlines are redrawn in black chalk.

It is difficult to tell whether the lower half of the sheet was originally drawn for the Maximilian project, or was made specifically to use Manet's banned composition in the new context of the Commune. At all events, Manet transformed the design into a scene of the Paris barricades, adding an upper sheet on which to sketch the architectural elements of his street scene. The ambitious scale of the drawing suggests that it may have been a project for a new Salon painting, but no painted version has been recorded. (Figs. 73 and 74.)

40. *La barricade*. c.1871.
Lithograph. 46.5 by 33.4 cm. An early, possibly contemporary, proof, before the posthumous edition of 1884.
Szépmüvészeti Múzeum, Budapest (1573.913).

From his *Barricade* drawing, Manet made a slightly smaller lithograph which, like that of the *Execution of Maximilian* (**34**), remained unpublished during his life-time. The composition is reversed and the schematic outlines of the soldiers, including the head without a body on the left, suggest that the print was made by means of a tracing, perhaps from a photograph of the drawing. In this early proof, the lines extend into the margins of the print, which is of exceptional richness. (Fig. 75.)

41. *Guerre civile*. 1871–73.
Lithograph. 39.9 by 58 cm. Signed and dated l.l. *Manet/1871*. Edition of 1874.
Department of Prints and Drawings, British Museum, London (1949.4.11.3336).

This is one of two lithographs published in 1874 (the other being an interpretation of the *Boy with a dog*, Fig. 17b). Here, the stark subject and the freedom and richness of the handling recall the treatment of similar themes by Daumier. Although Manet was prevented from showing scenes of execution – of the Emperor Maximilian in Mexico or of victims of the Commune in Paris – he paid homage to the dead, soldiers and civilians fallen together, in this moving design. (Fig. 76.)

Cafés-Concerts and the Folies-Bergère

42. Diagrammatic reconstruction of *Reichshoffen*. 1877–78.

Around 1877, Manet began work on a large Salon picture showing the interior of the Brasserie Reichshoffen, on the Boulevard Rochechouart. The café customers, some of them posed by Manet's friends, sat on either side of a table, with a window in the background, and a waitress serving mugs of beer on the right.

The composition was probably based on a drawing (**43**), see (b – d), and is known from two paintings which Manet cut from the large canvas and partially reworked. The section (a – 3) is now in Winterthur (**45**) and the section (3 – 2), with the later addition of a strip of canvas (2 – c), is in London (**46**).

Manet cut the large canvas in three places, first at (1) and (2), and finally, after rejoining (1), at (3). The left section went to a collector in Marseille. The right section remained in Manet's studio and was repainted, in several stages. It is shown here in the X-ray image which reveals the original design, with the continuation of the window which is still visible in the Winterthur picture.

The left (Winterthur) section extends beyond the limits of the composition seen in the drawing. Since the right section was cut at (2), there is no way of knowing how far it extended and where the right edge of the original *Reichshoffen* composition lay. (Fig. 77.)

43. *Café scene*. c.1877.
Lead pencil on a double page of a squared notebook. 14.2 by 18.7 cm. Annotated at right *blanc* and *rouge*.
Cabinet des Dessins, Musée du Louvre, Paris (RF 30.403).

This rapid sketch of a man and woman at a café table, seen against the light from a large window, was jotted down in a notebook as Manet observed the scene. It probably served as the basis of a very large composition (see **42**), now known from two pictures cut from the original canvas (**45** and **46**). (Fig. 79.)

44. 1883 photograph by Lochard, '*La servante de bocks*' (see **46**).
Photographic print mounted on card. 9.1 by 5.9 cm. (photograph) 29 by 20 cm. (card). Annotations by Léon Leenhoff.
Cabinet des Estampes, Bibliothèque Nationale, Paris (S.n.r. Manet, boîte 6).

This unique, unbound Lochard photograph card shows the London picture (**46**) photographed by Lochard in Manet's studio in 1883. The annotations by Léon Leenhoff correspond with the information given in his register of Manet's works, in which this painting is described as item 8. Besides recording the signature and date 1878 on the picture, the card indicates a date of 1877 for the work and names the people represented in the scene. (Fig. 80.)

45. Photograph of *Au café*. 1877–78.
Oil on canvas. 77 by 83 cm. Signed and dated l.r. *Manet/1878*.
Sammlung Oskar Reinhart 'Am Römerholz', Winterthur.

The painting is a relatively unchanged fragment of Manet's large *Reichshoffen* composition (see **42**). The figures of the actress Ellen Andrée and Manet's young engraver friend, Henri Guérard, are seen against the large café window whose right side appears in the X-ray images of the London fragment (**47**) and its Paris variant (**48**). Manet first cut through the *Reichshoffen* canvas just to the right of Guérard's head, so the right section of this picture was originally part of the London canvas (**46**). It may have been at this intermediate stage, when the cut canvas corresponded with section (1 – 2) of the *Reichshoffen* composition (**42**), that Manet added the girl in profile, who is painted over the original background. (Fig. 81. Col. ill. 4.)

46. *Coin de café-concert*. 1877–79.
Oil on canvas. 98 by 79 cm. Signed and dated l.r. *Manet/1878*(?).
The Trustees of the National Gallery, London (3858).

The painting, now known simply as *The waitress*, was once part of Manet's large *Reichshoffen* canvas (see **42**), from which he cut and reworked two fragments. To the right-hand fragment (**42**, 3 – 2), Manet added a wide strip of canvas (2 – c), and extended onto it the figures of the waitress and the man in the foreground. The change of colour in his blue smock clearly marks the new piece of canvas. The picture was sold to a M. Barroil from Marseille, who later exchanged it for the left-hand (Winterthur) painting (45). Back in Manet's studio, the London picture was further reworked and given a new background. The café-concert scene, with a dancer on stage and musicians below, was painted from sketches apparently made at a café-concert on the Champs-Elysées (50 and 51). Manet exhibited the completed painting in 1880, with the title *Coin de café-concert*. (Fig.82. Col.ill.5.)

47. X-radiograph of 46. Fragment of the *Reichshoffen* café scene (see 42), with an additional strip of canvas on the right. 1877–78.

The X-ray image shows how the London picture related to the Winterthur canvas before they were cut apart at (3) on the diagram (42). The light area at the left edge indicates the end of the window, which was later replaced by the café-concert scene. The original position of the waitress is just visible, with her head and white collar on the line where the two pieces of canvas are joined. The final placing of her head shows clearly, above the man in blue, with alterations to its shape that resulted in the painting out of the curls on her forehead, seen in the Paris picture (49). Changes in the position of the beer mugs held by the waitress and in the elbow, hand and pipe of the man in blue are also visible. The alterations and scraping of the canvas make the X-ray image confused and difficult to read, but it provides a great deal of information about the development of the painting. (Fig.83.)

48. X-radiograph of 49. *La serveuse de bocks*.

This X-ray image of the Paris picture (49) shows that it followed the underlying *Reichshoffen* composition, as seen in the X-ray of the London painting (47). The same light area on the left indicates the original café window and although the waitress is now in her 'final' position, above the man in blue, her soft, smiling features probably indicate her appearance in the original composition, where she appeared as a counterpart to Ellen Andrée in the Winterthur canvas (see 42 and 45). This canvas, which has been cut on all sides except at the right edge, was no doubt painted to help Manet redesign part of the cut *Reichshoffen* canvas (42, 1–2). (Fig.84.)

49. *La serveuse de bocks*. c.1878–80.
Oil on canvas. 77.5 by 65 cm. Inscribed l.r. *E.Manet*.
Musée d'Orsay – Galeries du Jeu de Paume, Paris (RF 1959.4).

In this picture, as in the London *Coin de café-concert* (46 and 47), Manet replaced the original Reichshoffen café window (see 42 and 45) by a café-concert scene, so that the young woman at the table looks at the entertainers rather than out of the window. The waitress and the man in a blue smock are in the positions adopted by Manet when he repainted the London canvas, altering the relationship of the figures and raising the man's hand and pipe to obscure the face of the figure next to him. Manet's final alterations to the Paris canvas changed the background (the underlying paint layers are visible at the top and left edges) and slightly altered the face of the waitress. (Fig.85. Col.ill.7.)

50. *At the café-concert*. c.1878–80.
Lead pencil with black chalk corrections. Double page of a squared notebook. 13.1 by 16.6 cm. Studio stamp l.r.
Cabinet des Dessins, Musée du Louvre, Paris (RF 30.526).

This rapid pencil sketch captures a view of the audience and some of the musicians who appear in the background of the London *Coin de café-concert* (46). The head of the boy in the foreground was added in black chalk over a vague pencil outline. (Fig.86.)

51. *Singer and musicians*. c.1878–80.
Lead pencil on a double page from a notebook. Smooth laid paper. 18.5 by 29.4 cm. Studio stamp l.l.
Cabinet des Dessins, Musée du Louvre, Paris (RF 30.402).

The musicians glimpsed in the small notebook drawing (50) reappear here, trombonist to the left, double-bass player to the right, while the unseen conductor's baton and score appear at the left edge, as in the London *Coin de café-concert* (46). These notebook drawings were made, according to Léon Leenhoff's notes, at a café-concert (probably an open-air establishment) on the Champs-Elysées (see 52). (Fig.88.)

52. *La belle Polonaise*. c.1879–80.
Brush transfer lithograph. 28.5 by 26.5 cm. Initialled l.l. *M*. Unique proof.
Cabinet des Estampes, Bibliothèque Nationale, Paris (Inv.71).

In this bold and witty design, the singer is the same chinless 'beauty' who appears in the background of the Baltimore *Café-concert* (53). Léon Leenhoff recorded, on a sheet that was probably an alternative preparatory drawing for this print, that she was a 'singer at a café-concert on the Champs-Elysées' (see Fig.91). The proof is unique and the lithograph was probably abandoned because the lower part of the singer's arms and body (seen in the drawing) failed to print. (Fig.92.)

53. X-radiograph of 54. *Café-concert*.

The extensive reworking of the background and the figure on the left make the X-ray difficult to read. But it shows a number of alterations to the objects in the foreground and explains the gesture of the man's left hand: it rested originally on a beer mug which Manet then moved to the right edge. In doing so, he also moved a tall glass with a spoon, which appears in the X-ray as a double image. (Fig.93.)

54. *Café-concert*. c.1878–80.
Oil on canvas. 47.5 by 39.2 cm. Signed l.l. *Manet*.
The Walters Art Gallery, Baltimore (893).

This small painting, about half the size of the London *Coin de café-concert* (46), has a freshness and brilliance which suggest that it was painted at one go. In fact, it turns out to have been altered almost as much as the London picture. It was developed along with the London and Paris paintings and at some stage the canvas was cut at the top and left edges and restretched. The original background, glimpsed at the top edge, was the same as in the Paris picture (49): dark red with a floral pattern and stripes. Manet tried out another background before reaching his final solution, with the blue-grey wall and the mirror image of 'la belle Polonaise' on stage, as she appears in the lithographic print (52). The woman seated on the left was originally dressed in black, and then in blue, before finally acquiring her drab beige dress. Only the man in the top hat was never retouched, and his face was brushed in very freely, with the bare, primed canvas showing. (Fig.94, Col.ill.6.)

55. *'La servante de bocks' (Café-concert)*. 1880.
Brush and ink with gouache. 25.5 by 21.5 cm. Signed l.l. *Manet*.
The Burrell Collection, Glasgow Museums and Art Galleries (35.312).

In April 1880, an exhibition of 'New works by Edouard Manet' was held at the gallery of *La Vie Moderne*. Among the ten paintings shown were the two café-concert scenes now in London and Baltimore (46 and 54). The exhibition was announced in the magazine *La Vie Moderne*, and after it had closed at the end of the month, the magazine published a postscript, on 8th May, in the form of a full-scale reproduction of this drawing based on the Baltimore *Café-concert* (54). The monochrome drawing, no doubt made with the line-block in view, has been 'corrected' in white gouache. (Fig.95.)

56. *Au paradis. (In the gods.)* 1877.
Brush transfer lithograph. 20.5 by 25.7 cm. (subject), 29 by 43.7 cm. (printed letters). Signed with initials l.r. *E.M.* Edition published in the *Revue de la Semaine* [April 1877].
Department of Prints and Drawings, British Museum, London (1949.4.11.3345).

This print, published in a weekly review in 1877, suggests that Manet was sketching in variety theatres as well as cafés at the time he began work on his ambitious *Reichshoffen* composition (42, 45 and 46). It shows a lively group of lads in the upper balcony of a theatre, and is very similar to a drawing based, according to Léon Leenhoff, on sketches made at the Folies-Bergère (Fig.97). The young men are gazing at a performance which, since they seem to be looking in various directions, could well be an act such as the Hanlon Lees brothers on their flying trapeze (58). (Fig.96.)

57. *Théâtre des Folies-Bergère*, by Barclay. 1875.
Water-coloured gillotage. Inscribed l.l. BARCLAY *Del.* and l.r.
LEFMAN *Sc.* 15.5 by 38.5 cm. (borderline).
Cabinet des Estampes, Bibliothèque Nationale, Paris (Va 286, XIII).

This theatre seating plan shows the interior of the Folies-Bergère. The view from the stage, framed by the curtain, shows the orchestra stalls and the ground floor boxes, and indicates the promenade running round behind them and a café at the back. Above, supported on slender columns, is the great gallery or circle, with its seats and then tiers of boxes. Here, too, there is a café and a promenade. The roof structure rests on broad pilasters against the gallery walls, to which gas-lit globes are attached. These, together with the decorated front of the gallery and the five great chandeliers, provide the elements of the setting for Manet's *Bar at the Folies-Bergère* (**60** and **62**). (Fig.99.)

58. *Folies-Bergère. Représentations des Frères Hanlon-Lees et de Little Bob, Gymnastes Américains*, by Beaurepaire after Truchon. November 1872.
Wood-engraving. 33.5 by 23.5 cm.
Cabinet des Estampes, Bibliothèque Nationale, Paris (Va 286, XIII).

The engraving shows the kind of performance that took place at the Folies-Bergère, with trapeze acts in the main body of the hall as well as pantomime and ballet on the stage. A poster advertising the celebrated Hanlon Lees team appears on the café window in the left half of Manet's *Reichshoffen* composition (**42** and **45**), and for many years they were one of the most popular acts at the Folies-Bergère. The little green feet which appear in the *Bar at the Folies-Bergère* (**62**) indicate such an act in progress. (Fig.100.)

59. X-radiograph of **60.** Sketch for *Un bar aux Folies-Bergère.*

The X-ray shows little evidence of changes beyond those already visible on the canvas surface: the high-necked and possibly long-sleeved dress, and the shift in the position of Dupray, at the right edge. (Fig.101.)

60. Sketch for *Un bar aux Folies-Bergère.* 1881.
Oil on canvas. 47 by 56 cm.
Stedelijk Museum, Amsterdam. On loan from Dr. F. F. R. Koenigs.

From his pencil sketches made at the Folies-Bergère, Manet painted this composition sketch in oils, in preparation for the large painting intended for the Salon of 1882. Léon Leenhoff noted that the barmaid from the Folies-Bergère is talking to Henry Dupray (a painter friend of Manet) in the studio on the rue d'Amsterdam. This probably applies to the underlying composition of the large *Bar*, as seen in its X-ray image (**61**), rather than to the swiftly and freely brushed sketch. In this sketch, the barmaid has a very blonde, very piled-up hairstyle (marked for reduction with a pencil line) and she originally wore a high-necked dress of Prussian blue. Dupray, eyeing her quizzically with his cane to his chin, appears to have been moved slightly down and to the right. The canvas was cut at the top and on the left, and Manet painted a new left end to the bar, within the new format. (Fig.102. Col. ill.8.)

61. X-radiograph of **62.** *Un bar aux Folies-Bergère.*

The X-rays of *Le déjeuner sur l'herbe* (**44** and **45**) and the *Bar* have revealed the most exciting discoveries so far made in Manet's major paintings. The X-ray image of the *Bar* shows how he began by painting onto the large canvas the precise design of the composition sketch (**60**). It makes 'sense' of all the incomprehensible – some have even said inept – elements of the final composition.

In the initial laying-in of the picture, although the barmaid was apparently centrally placed from the start, she was slighter. She stood with her arms crossed loosely in front of her and with her reflection in the mirror just behind and to the right, as in the sketch. Manet then moved her reflection to the right, in two stages, so that she first approached the figure of Dupray and finally obscured him altogether. Manet then added the figure of a top-hatted man in the upper corner, which confronts the girl's mirror reflection at very close quarters. Other changes in the picture, too numerous to mention here, can be seen by comparing the sketch and the final version of the Salon painting with this X-ray. (Fig.103.)

62. *Un bar aux Folies-Bergère.* 1881–82.
Oil on canvas. 96 by 130 cm. Signed and dated on the bottle label at the left *Manet/1882.*
The Home House Trustees, Courtauld Institute Galleries, London.

Suzon, one of the barmaids from the Folies-Bergère, posed for this painting in Manet's studio. In the sketch (**60**), she stands behind a black wooden bar probably seen at the theatre. Here, she poses behind a marble table-top, apparently a prop in Manet's studio, since it appears in the Baltimore *Café-concert* (**54**) and other late pictures. The end of the table-top is seen in the mirror, with the reflections of the foreground bottles made quite unrealistic by Manet's alterations to the picture (as seen from the X-ray image, **61**).

Behind the barmaid's improbably stocked bar (a superb still-life arranged by Manet for purely pictorial effect), is a view of the interior of the Folies-Bergère. Léon Leenhoff identified the setting as 'the bar on the first floor, to the right of the stage'. The theatre seating plan (**57**) shows how closely Manet kept to the real setting: the balcony with its seats and boxes, the broad pilasters with gas-lit globes, and the five great chandeliers.

Méry Laurent, a friend of Manet and Mallarmé, leans on the edge of the balcony, dressed in white. Behind her, the young actress Jeanne Demarsy appears in a box. The little green legs of a trapeze artist, perhaps one of the Hanlon Lees brothers (**58**), swing into sight in an upper corner. In the centre of the picture, the barmaid confronts her customer. But his reflection, and hers, have been moved so far away that in the end the viewer finds himself alone with the barmaid and her elusively averted gaze. (Fig.104. Col. ill.9.)

Bibliography

This brief bibliography of works cited in the text is preceded by a description of the documentary sources used. For a fuller bibliography, see the 1983 Paris/New York exhibition catalogue.

Documents

COPIE . . . DE DOCUMENTS. *Copie pour Moreau-Nélaton de documents sur Manet appartenant à Léon Leenhoff vers 1910.* Manuscript notebook. Cabinet des Estampes, Bibliothèque Nationale, Paris (Yb³ 2401).

The notebook includes: various letters and notes; the 'Carnet d'Edouard Manet', 1872–83 (lacking 1874–75); the 'Catalogue Manet 1884, Projet de Bazire'; the 'Petit carnet avec répertoire', including the 1872 sale to Durand-Ruel and studio inventory; and the 'Agenda de Manet 1883'. Most of the documents were used or quoted in MOREAU-NÉLATON [1926].

GODET, Photographs of paintings by Edouard Manet. Paris [1872]. Cabinet des Estampes, Bibliothèque Nationale, Paris (Dc 300a, vol. II). Twenty-four photographic prints registered by Godet with the Dépôt légal on 3rd April 1872, Nos. 851–874, *Oeuvres de Mr. Ed. Manet. 24 pl.* See the *États des Dépôts de la Librairie* (Ye 79).

Godet registered one photograph, *Le bon bock*, on 24th May 1873 (No. 1085) and another, *Nana*, on 15th May 1877 (also No. 1085). B.N. Paris (as above). Further prints are in the B.N. Paris (Dc 300f, 4 vols.) and in the Pierpont Morgan Library, New York (ex-Tabarant).

LÉON LEENHOFF, Register of works by Edouard Manet (paintings, pastels, drawings and prints) in his studio and in the collections of the Manet family and various friends and dealers in 1883. Manuscript. Cabinet des Estampes, Bibliothèque Nationale, Paris (Yb³ 4649; 4649a).

Notebook, with entries on pages numbered 1 to 307 (pages 138, 139, 307, 308 not used). The original pencilled entries were amplified in pen and ink, as on the Lochard photograph cards. The register numbers were used for the Lochard photographs.

LOCHARD, Photographs of works by Edouard Manet. 1883 (Nos. 1–307) and later. Cabinet des Estampes, Bibliothèque Nationale, Paris (Dc 300h, 1 vol.); Pierpont Morgan Library, New York (3 vols., ex-Tabarant).

Fernand Lochard's small photographic prints were mounted on cards and one complete set was numbered and annotated by Léon Leenhoff, in conjunction with the 'Register of works' (see above), and numbered above 327 for works photographed subsequently. These cards were bound, in haphazard order, in four volumes (B.N. Paris and New York).

At least two duplicate, mounted sets were made and bound, and Leenhoff's annotations were copied onto the cards (Bernheim-Jeune archives, Paris, eight albums). Further prints were mounted into other albums (B.N. Paris, Dc 300g, 8 vols.) and others are preserved loose (B.N. Paris, S.n.r. *Manet*, boîte; also includes the fully annotated, mounted print of the *Coin de café-concert*, see exh. cat. 44, Fig. 80). Further mounted photographs (probably from the Camentron set described by Tabarant) are also found in various collections. See TABARANT [1947], p. 518.

Catalogues raisonnés

RW see ROUART and WILDENSTEIN below.
LEIRIS see DE LEIRIS below.

Exhibition catalogues

Ingelheim [1977]
  Edouard Manet. Das Graphische Werk, by J. WILSON, ed. François Lachenal, Ingelheim am Rhein [1977].
Paris [1978]
  Manet: dessins, aquarelles, eaux-fortes, lithographies, correspondance, by J. WILSON, ed. Huguette Berès, Paris [1978].
Brown University [1981]
  Edouard Manet and the 'Execution of Maximilian', PAMELA M. JONES, et al., Brown University [1981].
Washington, D.C. [1982–83]
  Manet and Modern Paris, by T. REFF, Washington, D.C. [1982].
Paris/New York [1983]
  Manet, by F. CACHIN, C. S. MOFFETT, J. WILSON BAREAU, Paris and New York [1983].
London [1983]
  Manet at work, by M. WILSON, National Gallery, London.
Washington, D.C. et al. [1985–86]
  The Prints of Edouard Manet, by J. McK. FISHER, Washington, D.C. [1985].

Articles and monographs

E. BAZIRE: *Manet*, Paris [1884].
D. BOMFORD and A. ROY: 'Manet's "The Waitress": An Investigation into its Origin and Development', *National Gallery Technical Bulletin*, 7 [1983], pp. 3–19.
J. CORRADINI: *La Ninfa Sorprendida del Museo Nacional de Bellas Artes de Buenos Aires*, Buenos Aires [1983].
T. DURET: *Histoire d'Edouard Manet et de son œuvres*, Paris [1902].
B. FARWELL: 'Manet's "Nymphe surprise"', THE BURLINGTON MAGAZINE, CXVII [April 1975], pp. 224–29.
B. FARWELL: *Manet and the Nude: A Study in iconography in the Second Empire*, New York and London [1981].
A.-B. FONSMARK: 'Manet og Kejser Maximilians henrettelse. Om skitsen i Ny Carlsberg Glyptotek', *Meddelelser fra Ny Carlsberg Glyptotek*, 4 [1984], pp. 63–84.
E. M. GIFFORD: 'Manet's At the Café: Development and Structure', *The Journal of the Walters Art Gallery*, 42/43 [1984/85], pp. 98–104.
A. DE LEIRIS: *The drawings of Edouard Manet*, Berkeley [1969].
G. MAUNER: *Manet peintre-philosophe. A study of the painter's themes*, University Park (Pa.) and London [1975].
E. MOREAU-NÉLATON: *Manet raconté par lui-même*, Paris [1926].
A. PROUST: 'Edouard Manet. Souvenirs', *La revue blanche* [1897], pp. 125–35, 168–80, 201–07, 306–15, 413–24.
A. PROUST: 'L'art d'Edouard Manet', *Le Studio* [1901], pp. 71–77.
T. REFF: 'Manet and Blanc's "Histoire des peintres"', THE BURLINGTON MAGAZINE, CXII [July 1970], pp. 456–58.
T. REFF: see Exhibitions [1982].
D. ROUART and D. WILDENSTEIN: *Edouard Manet. Catalogue raisonné*, Geneva [1975].
A. TABARANT: *Manet. Histoire catalographique*, Paris [1931].
A. TABARANT: *Manet et ses œuvres*, Paris [1947].
J. WILSON: see Exhibitions [1977], [1978], [1983].
J. WILSON BAREAU: 'The portrait of Ambroise Adam by Edouard Manet', THE BURLINGTON MAGAZINE, CXXVI [December 1984], pp. 750–58.
M. WILSON: see Exhibitions, London [1983].

Index of lenders

Photographic credits

Unless otherwise indicated, all photographs come from the institutions named in the figure captions.

Studio P.Cadé, Paris,   90, 91, 97, 98
Courtauld Institute of Art, London   18, 44, 55, 67, 84
Doerner-Institut, Munich   70, 71
Galerie Hugnette Berès, Paris   34, 62, 72
Studio Lourmel-Photo Routhier, Paris   78
James Purcell/Musée d'Orsay, Paris   73, 74
Bruce Scott/Courtauld Institute, London   44
Fondation Wildenstein, Paris   43, 54